Chairs

a guide to choosing, buying and collecting

Chairs

a guide to choosing,
buying and collecting

Peter Darty

The Pyne Press
Princeton

This book is dedicated to Carolyn Russell

Drawings by Alan Spindler

Photography by Ken James

The author would like to thank the following people who allowed him to photograph and describe the chairs:

Mallett's, Sotheby's, Pelham Galleries, Hotspur, Dark and Rendlesham, Quercus, Gaye Maklin, Roslyn House Galleries, Phillips of Hitchin, Peter Bernard Ltd., Old Times, John Jesse, Adams Antiques, Angel Antiques, Keulamann, Victoria and Albert Museum and the American Museum at Bath.

The author would also like to thank Michael R. Carter, Carol Illingworth, Lydia Mottram, Susan Hawke and Diana Scarisbrick for their help.

SBN 87861-060-X

Library of Congress Catalog Card Number 73-91327

Filmset and printed in England by
Cox & Wyman Ltd, London, Fakenham and Reading

Contents

Introduction

Choosing and Buying Chairs

A chair can cost anything from 25p to £6,500, which was the price paid for the Medici throne in 1968, and if the throne in Westminster Abbey came on to the market, the price would be unimaginable. An important factor in paying a price for a chair is (*a*) to decide on its style (*b*) to note that it is originally that style (*c*) that it is a fine example of that style (*d*) that it is in good condition and that it has a mature and pleasant colour. A lack of a combination of these factors may vary the price of the article.

The actual price you pay will also depend on where you find the chair. If you buy it from a second-hand shop or small country sale the chances are that it will cost you less than if you find the same chair in one of the larger sale rooms in London, Paris or New York, or at an established antique dealer's. Even buying from these highly priced areas does not mean that you are not getting a chair that is a bad investment, as values change yearly, but a bad investment would be to buy a chair in a highly priced area without any knowledge or skill of what you are buying and then sell it in six months' time and expect a profit. That would be a bad risk, as furniture is not like stocks and shares which change daily. To invest, you should aim to buy a chair to use over the next couple of years and then to your delight find that it is worth more money than you originally paid for it, should you wish to sell it.

On the use of chairs—you must determine what its use is going to be—you don't use Chippendale chairs in the kitchen, unless you are extremely extravagant! There are particular types of chairs; for halls, dining-rooms, kitchens, studies, drawing-rooms, gardens, libraries—and chairs for many occupations such as cock fighting, lecture reading, nursing, commode chairs, invalid chairs, porters' chairs, campaign chairs, sedan chairs, and many others.

A chair and its value is only in the eye and the purse of the beholder. If you make a study of chairs and become involved in the subject, you will most probably find that your taste changes. This change is due to your increased knowledge in realising that there is a variety of choice, but the basic success of investing is that the object you buy purports to be what it is.

Advising on investment is difficult. Recent prices realised in the sale rooms and antique shops can be used only as a guide to the investor and should be treated as such. The advice and guidance of reliable and experienced dealers will be of invaluable help to the cautious buyer.

Advice on how to look and what to look for

One cannot learn the difference between oak, walnut and mahogany, or even what any of them look like, from a book. This can only be learnt by actually seeing the article. The look of timber varies over the ages and an experienced antique dealer can tell its age by looking at a piece of wood, in the same way that most people can tell the age of the design of clothes.

When asking about a chair, always ask what the wood is and what is its age, because the age will give you a clue to the style. Ask what the style is—ask how the chair is constructed—if it is constructed in a particular way, ask whether this is usual of the period. Notice the wear of use. Has the chair been repainted or revarnished at any time? Has it been repaired or even re-upholstered? Is the fabric period as well? (The latter is most unlikely.)

An important point to notice about any chair is the actual wear on the bottom of the legs—have they been cut down, have they been worn, is one worn and the other cut down to match? Have all the chairs in a set got strengthening butts or knees (angle blocks) under the seat. Notice the screws and see if they are hand made. Obvious points to look out for are modern screws, modern glues, modern nails, knees, differences in construction, i.e. strengthening, lack of wear in varnish and in woods, no paint crackle on lacquer furniture, sharp edges.

Grasp the seat firmly with one hand and the back with the other. There will be a slight movement but any rocking will indicate loose joints. Look at each leg in turn. Chair legs should match for grain and colour; any variation to this should be suspect and will suggest a replacement, perhaps from another chair. A new leg carefully matched to replace a broken one does not constitute a fake if it was done by a craftsman in the eighteenth or nineteenth century. If the new leg was put on recently it will certainly affect the value. An example of a fake is a piece of furniture made up in the particular style of a period in old wood by a craftsman. A point which applies to all woods is patina. The mellow tone in the colour of the wood comes from exposure to light and atmosphere, together with the effect of everyday use and many layers of polish or wax, which all go to make up the patina. This will be ruined if it is stripped off and french polished. The transparent surface built up on the wood over the years will disappear and no ammount of french polishing can replace a patina once removed. If the original surface has been removed, sound advice is to use a good quality wax on the natural wood and try to build up a patination, which, with time and care, will appear.

Look out for holes made by woodworm. Active worms provide dust as evidence and the holes will be light round the edges, while the holes of treated woodworm will be dark. Worm spreads very quickly to other pieces of furniture and should be treated immediately by fumigation or wood preservation.

In the past chairs were often repaired or strengthened with iron plates, which was done from either lack of knowledge or laziness. A skilled craftsman can repair chairs without the use of plates, and where they have been used, the best advice is to remove them completely and repair the chairs in the proper manner with proprietory products easily obtainable.

Having bought and repaired your chairs and turned them into things of beauty, have them insured against all risks (including floods) by an expert in the field along with your other furniture.

Chapter 1
English Chairs

The Gothic World

Gothic seats reflect the status of the sitter. In the fifteenth and sixteenth centuries the chair was often high backed with arms, and virtually unmoveable. Architectural in design, it stood in a place of honour for the Master of the household and occupied a permanent place on the wall side of the table, where it replaced the dormant chair constructed as part of the panelling with a canopy overhead. The stool and bench were common. The stool being often of triangular form, round or rectangular was constructed with two boards, the outer edges being formed or carved like buttresses with a seat on the top. The apron pieces were tenoned into board ends to give stability. These stools were plain with little decoration and were made out of oak, as was the bench, of which the ends were usually framed or panelled, the stiles being carried downwards to form feet.

Gothic architecture achieved something quite revolutionary in construction. Combining form and beauty, the builders of the Gothic world found that using the pointed arch with its balance of thrust and counter-thrust overcame a great constructional problem of how to enclose space with less material and less weight. Good examples are to be found at Chartres in France and at King's College Chapel, Cambridge. Usually, design in furniture follows the style of architecture, though in Gothic times it was found unnecessary to use the constructional ideas of the architecture, which meant that the furniture maker could rely on the use of beam and post, and use the pointed arches and tracery as a means of decorating the pieces that he

Two stools. Left, balluster shape. Right, columnar, ring turnings.
1630

Carved oak arm chair Bobbin turnings, decorated rail, panels and crest rail.
1640–1650

made. Little Gothic furniture has survived, and that which has is usually coarse and heavy in construction and ecclesiastical in form. The many illuminated manuscripts that survive depict furniture from everyday life in Gothic times with which the wealthy surrounded themselves. The construction of this furniture was from planks, usually of oak, trimmed with adzes and made up by carpenters who joined the pieces together with roughly made nails. Towards the end of the Gothic period framing and panelling became more widespread and the use of joints came on to the scene. The use of these enabled the furniture maker to abandon the use of large planks of wood for fronts, sides and tops. Horizontal rails and vertical stiles were mortised and tenoned together enclosing a thin panel of wood. Wooden pegs were driven into holes bored on the outside of the stile and through the tenon of the rail.

It can be seen that furniture made in this manner is naturally lighter in appearance and more portable. The use of panelling went further than chairs and coffers. In many houses it was used to decorate the walls. The word "wainscot" used today to describe this panelling referred originally not to the panelling or its construction, but to the particular type of oak from which it was made. In various accounts and inventories the term is applied to ordinary moveable furniture as well as the wall panelling. One result of the use of the panel was the box-like chair which was probably derived from the chest. It had panels at the side, back and under the seat with no legs. The arms being provided by flat rails on the side of the seat. It was made from the end of the fifteenth century until the late sixteenth century.

James I arm chair. Lozenge
decoration.
1640–1650

Cromwellian chair cum table in oak.
1650

The panels were at first decorated in the Gothic style with
tracery and linen-fold pattern the latter being common in the
second half of the fifteenth and early part of the sixteenth century.

The joiner was destined to play an important part in the
development of seat furniture. Chair making, until the end of
the Georgian period, was always regarded as a specialised form
of joinery. Long after the joined chair in its original form
became obsolete, the joiner kept the spirit and tradition of the
"Chair of State" alive by making ceremonial chairs for the
Court, various Ambassadors and the Inns of Court.

By the sixteenth century the Italian Renaissance style had
begun to reach Northern Europe, though it was not to establish
itself in England until the reign of Henry VIII. The English
craftsmen did not really understand its classical forms and
mixed it with the traditional Gothic styles. Henry VIII, until
his break with Rome, had encouraged Italian craftsmen, but
Reformation England was to a large extent kept out of direct
contact with Italy and the changes in decorative and constructional techniques in craftsmanship brought by the classical
Renaissance. Cultural contacts were closest with Protestant
countries such as Germany and the Low Countries where the
Renaissance style was interpreted as a rather complex and
ornate version of the original, but it appealed to the English
taste of the time. After the dissolution of the monasteries in
1534, a new class of landowners arose from the sale of the
monastic estates. Building activity was now centered on private
houses and no longer on the churches. This condition also
affected furniture styles, and there was increased output by

Box-shaped arm chair, first half
sixteenth century. Oak. Victoria and
Albert Museum.

3

Cromwellian wing arm chair. Oak framed, original leather upholstery.
1640

Charles I chair (one of a set of ten at Hardwicke Hall).
1640

craftsmen to furnish these new houses which rose on the skyline. The craftsmen, until the Reformation, had spent their time and skill satisfying the Church's needs, but with the abolition of the monasteries there was a decline in standards. After the death of Henry VIII, the Renaissance style was absorbed into the native Gothic style and England now began to exchange an almost medieval way of life for something novel. The new landowners, like new rich of all countries and eras, were undisciplined in their tastes and were the slaves of fashion, and to be fashionable you had to be Italianate. The styles which appealed to the Englishman in the mid-century often came from the alluring plates of the pattern books from the printing presses of Zurich, Antwerp and Nuremberg, which were crowded with ill-understood and superficial Renaissance themes. The most celebrated of these books were those published by Vredeman de Vries (1527 to 1604) published in Antwerp in about 1580. It was from these foreign sources that the most well known of Tudor ornaments were derived—strapwork, inlay and bulbs of grotesque proportions. The furniture remained mainly medieval in shape, gradually absorbing the new styles.

Flemish influence was increased with the arrival of craftsmen from the Netherlands who fled from religious persecutions. Almost the only articles of furniture that were improved in construction and design during the English Renaissance were chairs and stools. In the middle years of the century luxury was still associated with the use of richly decorative fabrics and leather hangings imported from Spain, and as in medieval

Mid-seventeenth-century oak arm chair. Thistle decoration.
Mid-seventeenth-century oak stool with unusual apron.

North country chair.
1660

times, the large panelled chair in a conspicuous position was reserved for the master of the house. The rest of the family sat on stools and benches of oak resting their backs against the wall.

It was during the sixteenth century that lighter forms of chairs came into fashion. One such chair was the *Caquetoire*, of possible French origin. It had a tall, narrow back and open sides. The carved decoration on the back often took the form of a lozenge enclosing a woman's head, and was surrounded by carved foliage. There are many chairs of a similar design in continental museums. Another lighter form of chair was the so-called *Glastonbury* type. Originating in Northern Italy, it had a raked back and arms shaped underneath that sloped upwards to support the elbows. Today there are similar chairs found in chancels of country churches in England.

The traditional panel-back chair is a good example of the changes which had occurred by the end of the century. The heavy clumsy version became lighter as the joiner gained experience in design and techniques. The arms, instead of being enclosed, are now open and scroll downwards in the centre for the sitter's elbow, and scrolled outwards over the arm supports. The front legs and arm supports were turned in columnar and other shapes. Often the back panels were carved or inlaid with coats of arms, sometimes with scrolled sections at the top and sides. Lighter chairs began to appear towards the end of the sixteenth century and one in particular was the back stool, which had a back but no arms, and was based on the joint stool which had four turned splayed legs. Its development coincided with the fashion for houses to have a separate dining-room, doing away with the great hall and its formal atmosphere when the master and mistress sat on a raised dais at the end of the hall. In the new small dining-room, life was much more cosy and homely, and some of the formalities were done away with. The table was in the centre of the room, and it has been suggested that the back stool was designed to take the place of the wall as support. By the time of the reign of Elizabeth I, upholstered seating was gradually becoming more fashionable and many elaborate chairs were produced for the great houses of the time. Many of them were in the traditional "X"-frame shape and were often completely covered in velvet. Few of these chairs survive, but in the Victoria and Albert Museum and in Winchester Cathedral there are examples. In the latter there is an oak chair covered in velvet made in about 1550 and said to have been used for the marriage of Mary Tudor to Philip II of Spain.

By the seventeenth century the upholsterer had begun to extend his range and richly upholstered chairs and stools of the Elizabethan style continued to be made. At first in the early seventeenth century some of the "X"-frame chairs had their whole frames covered with fringed velvet or silk and satin. These were fastened with brass-headed nails. The settee was a large chair broad enough to take two or three people. Some settees had iron ratchets attached to the adjustable ends, converting them into day beds. Day bed and couch were names used in the sixteenth and seventeenth centuries. The name sofa, of Arabic origin, was not in use until the eighteenth century.

One extraordinary chair which evolved during the reign of James I was the Farthingale chair. It was an upholstered single chair probably made to accommodate the extreme Spanish fashion for the whale bone hoop on which women's skirts hung. This made it difficult for the wearer to sit down in an arm chair, so all that was left was the stool or the back stool. These chairs were made all through the seventeenth century and were often covered with turkey-work wool on a canvas base, imitating turkey carpets. Some were covered in leather. They were often sold by the dozen and could also be hired when extra seating was needed. Their legs and stretchers were usually plain, but the legs were sometimes of columnar form. Upholstered chairs were usually of beech or walnut, but the original type of joined chair with panelled back and open arms was usually made of oak and made in country districts up until the eighteenth century.

Around 1650 a local form of chairs evolved. They were made in Northern England and were often called Yorkshire and Derbyshire chairs. Backs were either of an arcading of turned balusters on a centre rail or of two carved flat hooped rails.

The reigns of James I, 1603 to 1623, and Charles I, 1623 to 1649, brought about the introduction of classical architecture by Inigo Jones, who followed the architectural style of Andrea Palladio, though it had little effect on furniture. Charles I was one of England's most cultured monarchs and built up one of

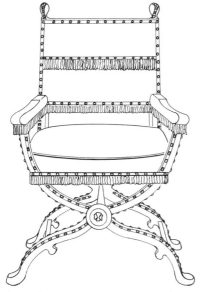

Arm chair of "X"-frame shape, the frame-work covered with fabric secured with ornamental studding. Early seventeenth century

Charles II arm chair in walnut.
Elaborate carving with cabriole legs.
cane back and seat.

English broadseated upholstered chairs. Bobbin and reel turning.
1650–1660

the finest art collections in Europe. He also took a great deal of
interest in the furnishings of the royal palaces. During the Civil
War, which broke out in 1642, the royal collections were
dispersed and much of the upholstered furniture suffered.
London at the beginning of the seventeenth century was becoming the chief furniture-making centre. In 1632, after a long
dispute about the functions and responsibilities of joiners,
turners, carpenters, and carvers, the London Guild of Carpenters and Joiners came to the agreement which, in effect,
gave the joiners the monopoly of making furniture with mortise
and tenons and dove-tail joints. This agreement was always
kept, but the joiners' supremacy was no longer in doubt. From
this time chair making became a specialised branch of joinery,
and remained so.

Austerity in style was the main theme of puritan England
under Cromwell and if no record of the Commonwealth Period
has survived, the character of the chairs alone give an idea of
the austere scene in the mid-seventeenth century. When the
Puritans ruled the country, those civilised people who could
afford to left to live abroad. Those who remained at home lived
cautiously, avoiding conspicuous clothes, furniture and possessions. The chairs with their leather seats and backs had an
austere air to them and brass-headed nails held the leather in
place. These were functional but were also decorative. Turners
and carvers indulged in a form of decoration that was evidently
approved of, reel and bobbin turning and ball turning, which
gave a decoration to the legs of the chairs. Ball bobbin and ring
turning had been practised for centuries, but throughout the

Charles II walnut wing arm chair. Later needlework upholstery.
1660–1670

William and Mary stool. Crossed serpentine stretchers. Walnut.
1690

Joined stool. The most common form of seating in Elizabethan England. Oak.
1600

Commonwealth Period this form of work was lavished on chair legs and stretchers, and the twist gradually evolved—hand carved at first, though after the Restoration the spiral twist became common. This technique was probably developed and perfected during the middle years of the century. The twist had been used in Spain and Flanders for legs of chairs and tables before it appeared in England, and like other ornamental themes, was the result of architectural inspiration. This style of leg was used a good deal after the reign of Charles II in 1660, and demonstrates how accomplished the art of turning had become. The double twist was an inevitable development and was used on all types of furniture legs.

During the Puritan rule the transition from the back stool or side chair (or single chair) was accomplished, and from then onwards the term "Arming Chair" or arm chair was used, as *chair* had become the accepted name for a seat of any kind. The term arm chair is first documented in the seventeenth century but it was probably used earlier. The term Carver Chair was first used in the nineteenth century—it distinguished the elbow chairs used at each end of the table from the armless dining chair. In the reign of Elizabeth I a set of upholstered chairs of a remarkably similar design had been in use. Suites became fashionable later in the seventeenth century and sometimes consisted of twenty-four chairs and stools and two, three or four couches. The design was related to the interior decoration of the salon, bringing continuity to the general scheme. They were also used in England in galleries and drawing-rooms in the eighteenth century.

Charles II country chair (Yorkshire). Completely original. End of the seventeenth century

William and Mary japanned carved high-backed elbow chair. Cabriole legs, caned back panels and seat. Shaped under stretchers. 1690

One of a pair of Queen Anne country chairs in fruitwood. 1710

Naturally the Puritan period brought a decline in the luxury trades and it was time of make-do and mend for many people, and as velvet and rare brocades were no longer available the wood of the chairs began to acquire a significance in style and decoration that was to remain for two hundred years. With no foreign influence the chair makers gained confidence in themselves and, when the French, Dutch and Oriental fashions arrived later in the seventeenth century, they were able to absorb these ideas and adapt them to English taste.

Restoration

The Restoration marked a reaction against eleven years of Puritan rule. The exiled royalists returned from the Continent with a taste for luxury which England had not known before, acquired from France where many of them had lived, and so it was from France that the chief foreign influence came. Louis XIV was fast becoming the leader of artistic taste in Europe. Trade with Holland and the arrival of Dutch immigrants, who came over with William and Mary, all helped to inspire new ideas in England. The great fire of London in 1666 destroyed much of the solid oak furniture, which had to be replaced. Walnut became the fashionable wood; two types were used, gold and dark brown, the latter coming from Virginia. Fortunes were spent on furnishing houses and many different coloured unusual woods such as coromandel and laburnum imported from the East and West Indies were used.

Pair of William and Mary chairs. Twist turn supports and stretchers. Crested stretchers. Interlaced strapwork. Painted beech.
1690–1700

Walnut and parcelgilt love seat.
1725

Chairs in the Charles II period were often made of walnut or beech, and their backs as well as their seats were caned. The caned back panels were supported by uprights which were turned and connected by a cresting rail tenoned between them. Caned chairs were first produced in England and Holland in about 1665 and gradually replaced the more expensive turkey-work chairs. At the time of the Restoration a low oblong back was popular on chairs. They looked rather like the chairs pictured in the paintings of Dutch interiors of that time, except that they did not have the spiral twists which were used after 1665. A combination of spiral and ball turning was used for legs and stretchers, and frame caning took the place of leather, velvet and turkey-work. Chairs were said to be "turned all over" and were often made in sets of two arm chairs and six single chairs. The turner played quite a large part in the construction and decoration of chairs. From the first few years of the new reign, backs of chairs were higher and had carving which was rather shallow with the royal crown flanked sometimes by two cherubs called Boyes and Crownes which was supposed to suggest a happy Restoration. Other themes were eagle's heads, fruit and flowers. After about 1665 a flat front stretcher rail was carved to correspond with the cresting rail. Many of the grander chairs showed a marked continental influence. Some chair seats were dished to take a squab cushion—the front legs projected above the seat to support the cushion. Chair arms at this time were usually scrolled. Many chairs of the plainer sort were made out of beechwood which was painted black to look like walnut. A number of these chairs survive today. Beautiful

One of a pair of Queen Anne walnut arm chairs covered in contemporary Soho tapestry. Arched and waisted back and saddle-shaped seats.

One of a pair of sofas in the style of William Kent. Cabriole legs and claw feet. 1730

damasks and figured velvets were used to cover chairs in the grander houses.

Chairs in the latter years of Charles II reign seemed to be much more elaborate—by this time the English craftsmen had come to terms with the new style and were able to produce anything that was required. There is a difference in the carving; the early carving was on solid ground, but now pierced work became popular and the frame of the panel as well as the cresting rail and front stretcher were carved in this way. After 1670 baluster turning which was so popular with sixteenth-century craftsmen, was revived and often replaced the spiral twist. The front legs were frequently scrolled and the ornamental scroll form became a prominent feature. By 1685 another prominent feature arose, that of an arched cresting replacing the earlier square shape. This was supported by the uprights instead of being tenoned into or between the square. The scrolled Portuguese front stretcher was sometimes used in combination with inward-turning scroll feet. Backs were often narrower and very tall, and the seats were supported on cupped legs linked by serpentine "X" stretchers with an ornamental finial in the middle.

Day Beds had been known in Tudor times but they came into fashion during the Restoration. They were carved and caned and often had adjustable ends. Squab cushions were supplied for comfort. The wing chair was introduced during the reign of Charles II, though very few survive. However, there are a wonderful pair at Ham House called Sleeping Chairs, which are carved and gilded and covered in a beautiful original

Queen Anne wing chair.
Contemporary needlework
upholstery. Knee-hipped, double-
pad foot. Walnut.

One of a set of four George I walnut
chairs. Ball and claw feet, uprights
and splat veneered. Eighteenth-
century needlework.
1725

Detail of crisply carved eagle's
head on knee.

brocade. The backs are fitted with adjustable iron ratchets.
The wings on these early chairs were called lugs or cheeks
and gave protection from the draught. Arms were either open
or padded. They were the ancestors of the easy chair and helped
to change the attitude to the standard of comfort which would
be demanded in the future. Upholstered chairs came into general
use, but they are scarce today and would be an expensive
investment. They were often covered in velvet or needlework
and must have looked very luxurious. They were sometimes
copies of French chairs and were carved and gilded in the
French manner.

Oak was used in the country districts during the early years
of the Restoration. The chairs had oak panelled backs and
looked rather austere, although on some of the later examples
the carving was elaborate. It is usual to find the back panel
set high above the seat with spiral twist uprights on each side.

The stool was still used as a customary seat and was made
out of walnut or beech and was often caned. After 1675 they
were upholstered. These were used side by side with the plainer
ones which had wooden seats and turned baluster legs. For the
wealthy, stools were supplied as part of the set of seating
furniture or were made to match the state beds. They varied in
shape, usually being square or rectangular. They developed at
the same time as the chair, and corresponded to the design
exactly. Stools were covered with an identical fabric and
embroidered with gold and silver thread. Front legs and
stretchers were usually carved. At court and on occasions of
ceremony it was fashionable for notables to sit on arm chairs

One of a set of four George I needlework-covered
mahogany arm chairs, each with a rectangular back.
The inswept arm supports faced with chains of husks
on a pitted ground and raised on short cabriole legs,
the back legs cabriole with broad pad feet.

Porter's chair.
Mid-eighteenth century.

accompanied by the guest of honour whilst the other guests
sat on stools.

William and Mary (1689 to 1702)

Furniture of the William and Mary period was influenced by
the Dutch and by a further influx of Dutch cabinet makers who
came to England after the accession of William. At the beginning
of the reign chairs were generally lighter in form and weaker in
construction, although at this time chairs of many styles and
designs existed. Some of the tallest chairs ever made in England
appeared in this reign. Chairs with turned uprights, turned
legs and stretchers and sometimes a double twist support were
made at the same time as those with crossed stretchers, often
surmounted by a finial. These were used in conjunction with the
straight legs which had been revived in about 1690. These
legs, sometimes baluster shape, and turned and tapering, were
headed by a square bulbous capping of mushroom- or pear-
shape and had fluting and gadrooning. Small shaped aprons
appeared on the seat rails of chairs at about this time.

Tall upholstered chairs without arms were designed with
rectangular backs. Occasionally, tops were shaped and woodwork was frequently gilded. A rich velvet was used as a covering.
Upholstered wing chairs were made throughout this period.
Those dating from the end of the century often had padded
scrolled arms and legs with pear-shaped cappings on the legs.

At the end of the century a new type of chair described as

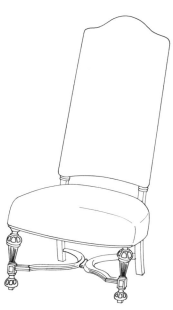

William and Mary chair of 1690,
carved and gilded with fluted baluster
legs which have mushroom cappings
and "X"-shaped stretchers.

13

Suite of George II carved mahogany hall furniture comprising two settees and four arm chairs. 1755–1758

Suite of George II carved mahogany hall furniture comprising two settees and four arm chairs. 1755–1758

Farthingale chair, early seventeenth century

in the style of Daniel Marot made its appearance. Marot, who came from a Huguenot family of architects and designers, was driven from France by the persecution that followed the revocation of the Edict of Nantes in 1685. He became the architect to William of Orange (later William III). He did extensive work at Hampton Court, both on the furniture and the interior decoration, and had considerable influence on design during the first few years of the eighteenth century. The type was distinctive and in several features foreshadowed coming fashions. A narrow back of curved outlines, which often enclosed a vase or fiddle-shaped back. In imitation of French and Italian chairs, legs were cabriole at the front. Some of these chairs can be seen at Hampton Court.

There was a great fashion for lacquering or lacquered furniture imported by the East India Company. This fashion spread with the publication in 1688 of *A Treatise of Japanning* by John Stalker and George Parker, and naturally the publication of such a book gave reign to the keen amateur as well as the professional. Green, red, blue and yellow were used and often in Chinese motifs. Few chairs of this style survive.

Queen Anne (1702 to 1714)

During the reign of Queen Anne, 1702 to 1714, furniture styles showed a gradual development of fluidity of line and comfort. Simplicity, sound construction and elegant lines unite to produce some of the most popular furniture ever made in England. The

Hall chair (one of a set of four).
Mid-eighteenth century

George III two-chair backed settee. Gothic-style back, straight legs, under
stretchers, lift-out seat.
1760

period was remarkable for its newly awakened appreciation of
form, a style which replaced the elaborate and decorative themes
of the previous periods. Lavish ornament was banished in
favour of smooth, gentle contours. Beauty of surface remained
with the use of decorative veneers of walnut and other woods.
Delicate carving in low relief replaced the flamboyant carving
of the William and Mary period. Shape and line of furniture
became more curvilinear in conception. This is seen particularly
in the Queen Anne chair, which replaced the rather flimsy cane
chairs of William and Mary. Instead of being designed for upright posture, the Queen Anne chair was produced to fit the
contours of the sitter's back, a production of skill and restraint,
known at the time as the bend-back chair. Back uprights rose
from slightly splayed back legs. The fronts of the uprights and
splat were often veneered with walnut. The back splat was vase
shape in form and later, fiddle shape. Use of the cabriole leg
freed the leg from support of the necessary stretchers, though
at first it was retained. The cabriole legs followed a broad structural evolution, at first relatively narrow and square in section,
then gradually assumed greater width and strength, but a
delicately carved shell appeared on the knee. The origin is something of a puzzle. Statement suggests its source as Chinese
or Dutch or the back hock of an animal. The *pied de Biche*
(deer foot) was one of the earliest to be used with the cabriole
leg, followed by the pad foot, and after about 1710 the ball and
claw (said to be derived from an Eastern source of a dragon
holding a precious jewel). The pony hoof was another form
still used in 1730. By 1714, with the advent of the hanoverians

One of a set of four Chippendale chairs. An interesting model, as the splat has a Chinese flavour. Square leg and under stretchers. 1760–1765

there was a revival of ornament. The cresting of the chair had a new form of carving in the suggestion of leather or strapwork. The simple shell became stylised in design and was often used on the hip of the legs. The settee had been introduced in the seventeenth century, and by Queen Anne's reign, designs for settees and wing chairs were more uniform. The wings on chairs finished in padded arm rests with an outward scroll. The arms and wings appeared in one continuous curve, presenting a pleasing line. Another chair with graceful lines and contours was the upholstered Queen Anne chair with arms continuing to looped terminals on curved supports. The back of this chair was reduced in height. Settees with open arms or closed sides and settees with two or three chair backs remained in fashion throughout the century.

The Eighteenth Century

During the eighteenth century cabinet making reached its zenith. At no time since has design and construction been so closely affiliated. By the middle of the century there was a large and complex organisation of workshops situated in the neighbourhood of St Martin's Lane, Soho and St Paul's Churchyard. Chair making in the eighteenth century became a specialised trade. Chairs from England were copied all over the world and Chippendale designs could be found in America and Europe. By the end of the century the Neo-classical style had a wider influence. It was the age of the "Enlightened Patron", who, by doing the Grand Tour had gained a knowledge and a feeling for the classical tradition, and was aware of other arts and styles of Europe. The architects of the time achieved a harmony, unknown before, between meticulously designed interior schemes and furniture designed to harmonise with the whole theme. Cabinet makers of the eighteenth century had a feeling for design and a choice of rare and beautiful woods from all over the world to work with.

A change in taste and style made itself apparent after the death of Queen Anne, and there appeared a more ornate form of decoration for chairs. They tended to become more heavy in form, though still made in the curvilinear style. In the early years of George I, 1714 to 1727, the most characteristic features of chairs were human and animal motifs that formed the main decorative theme. By 1720 mahogany was beginning to supplant walnut as the most fashionable wood. The heavy duty levied on imported timbers from America and the West Indies was abolished by an Act of Parliament in 1721. Prices fell and timber merchants exploited woods from the West Indies, mahogany being one of them. Jamaica was the main source for supply, though it was also imported from the islands of San Domingo and Cuba. Mahogany appears to have been first used for chair making around 1725, but as mentioned, it

Pair of Chippendale country ladderback chairs in mahogany.
1760

Chippendale chair in the Gothic
style. Unusual leg.
1755

had been used for other furniture at an earlier date. Mahogany,
a superb material, hard and close grained, was ideal for carving
and took a high polish. The change-over from walnut as the most
fashionable wood took time, and it was still being used in
mid-century. Chairs made in mahogany resembled their walnut
counterparts at first, though Spanish mahogany (which came
from San Domingo) had very little figuring to the grain and it
was mostly used in the solid and not as a veneer. The wood
lent itself to carving in a crisp and vigorous manner and the
plain austere feeling of the dark wood was soon relieved by
decorative carved details.

The solid splat of the earlier chairs now became pierced. The
years between 1720 and 1730 brought about a drop in the height
of the chair and the use of lion's head mask carved on the legs
and as a terminal figure to the arms. Legs ended in a realistically
carved lion's paw or claw and ball foot. The eagle and bird motif
was another favoured by the carvers of the day. Legs were also
carved with leaf, cabochon motif and human or satyr mask.
Carving was carried out with style and skill on the cresting rails,
splats and aprons of the chairs. An interesting feature was the
hipped cabriole leg when the leg was extended to join the seat
rail. Chair shapes were heavier in form, seats often much wider
and backs lower. The arm supports were no longer taken
straight from the leg to the arm, but were set back on the side
rails. Arms were curved to fit the elbows and scrolled over the
supports and the back splat was widened. Upholstered chairs
with low backs and wide seats were made to accommodate the
full-bottomed coats and wide hoops of the fashions of the time.

One of a set of four mahogany chairs. Serpentine cresting rail with honeysuckle motif in centre splat.

Hall chair. Saddle seat with family crest painted on the back. 1770

Hall chair. Saddle seat with family crest painted on the back. 1770

Some chairs were gilded to match the large side tables in the ornately decorated room of the period.

It was William Kent who exemplified this rather grand Baroque style. Kent was the first English architect to include interior decoration in the overall design for his interiors. He had studied in Italy, where he met Lord Burlington who became his patron. Architecture of the exterior of houses designed by Kent was in the restrained manner of the Palladian revival; though for the interiors he favoured the rather grand and monumental style that he had seen on his travels in Italy from 1710 to 1719 where he studied painting. He made great use of gilt and parcel gilt. Some of the elaborate chairs he designed can be seen at Holkham Hall, Norfolk, a house in the Palladian style that he designed for Sir Robert Walpole. The gilt was applied on a ground of gesso, a chalk and parchment size which covered pine or beech and was then carved in low relief. The fashion for gilding was at its height in the first quarter of the century. The decoration of these chairs was often of lion's masks, acanthus scrolls and many classical motifs. Combined with brilliantly coloured upholstery the furniture looked ostentatious and was well suited to the interiors for which it was designed. The interiors of the Palladian house were designed in the Italian style. The main rooms on the first floor were called the Piano Nobile, the long gallery being replaced by the Library and Saloon where naturally particular pieces of furniture were required, and this brought about the introduction of various types of library chairs and reading chairs. They often had three legs at the front and one at the back, and some-

A fine pair of English late-eighteenth-century arm chairs with cabriole legs, decorated in white and gold.

One of a set of six Sheraton mahogany chairs. 1795

Rococo with straight legs, apparently preferred for the dining-room. Chippendale's upholstered French chairs with elbows, based on Louis XV Fauteuils (in fact he imported them to copy) had cartouche-shaped backs, exposed frames carved with Rococo foliage and cabriole legs with the French whorl foot, representing a successful attempt at Anglo–French curvilinear design. At this time the outscrolled arms of upholstered settees became higher and formed a continuation of an undulating back, a fashion borrowed from Louis XV Canapés.

The term Country Chippendale describes the simplified and often improved versions from *The Director*, taken by rural craftsmen who were content to imitate the plain square sectioned back, legs and stretchers. These country craftsmen invented the wheatsheaf and lancet back; the wheatsheaf had pierced and waisted splat, and the lancet was in the Gothic taste. The splat and piercings were not as elaborate in the country-made pieces, and the legs were usually plain and straight. Woods were usually walnut, oak and fruitwoods. These country pieces have never been copied, whereas the more stylish models have been reproduced, so any country models will be original, if difficult to date.

The Director was the first book on furniture to be produced by a cabinet maker and it was, as can be expected, followed by many others in the same vein. William Ince and John Mayhew started to issue in separate parts *The Universal System of Household Furniture*, published in 1759 at one shilling each. However, in 1763 it appeared in book form. It included a number of designs for chairs similar to those in *The Director*,

Cromwellian arm chair with sloping back, from the Wingfield Castle collection. 1640–50

A Hepplewhite beechwood arm chair in the French manner. *Circa* 1770

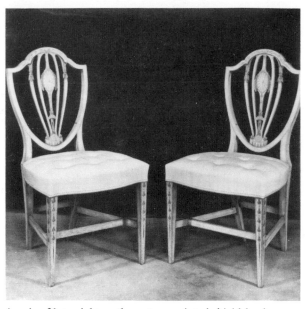

A pair of late-eighteenth-century painted shield-back single chairs.
1765

some in the Chinese taste, French chairs, dressing chairs, single chairs with upholstered seats and backs called back stools, two half couches called burjars or birjairs (bergère was a French name for an upholstered arm chair). This form of chair was used by Sheraton in his *Cabinet Dictionary*, published in 1803. These were caned at the back and under the arms. *The Cabinet and Chair Maker's Real Friend and Companion*, was published in 1765 by Robert Manwaring. It repeats Chippendale's advice about the study of architecture and illustrates the classic orders. The book has some hundred designs on forty plates, and many of the chairs shown in it could easily have been adapted from Chippendale's *The Director*, though Manwaring claimed that they were originals and included Chinese and Gothic chairs and also ten designs for rural chairs, which he states are for summer houses, gardens and parks. These seats for outdoor use were often made to match natural surroundings and some were carved to simulate the trunks and branches of trees.

Robert Adam

The fashion for Rococo was on the wain by the time of the accession of George III in 1760, even though in the third edition of *The Director*, Chippendale had included mostly Rococo themes, but as with all fashions they had had their day. People had become bored with the asymmetrical intricacies of the Rococo style—the discovery of Pompeii and Herculaneum had created an interest in classical forms. It was Robert Adam, who, after

A late-eighteenth-century mahogany shield-back single chair with carved splat.

One of a set of six Hepplewhite- and Sheraton-style chairs. Prince of Wales feathers.
1785

Detail of reeded leg with spade foot.

studying classical design in Italy and Dalmatia between 1754 and 1758, was to influence his generation with the spirit of the Neo-classical style, which he interpreted in an individual manner. No cabinet maker was untouched by his influence. He was an architect who was not only responsible for the exterior, but undertook the complete interior decoration and designing of fittings, etc. For many years it was thought that he originated the Neo-classical style, but recent research shows that in fact Sir William Chambers and James Stuart, both architects, had made excursions into this style by designing furniture. It is also interesting to try and relate the style in France to that in England, but up to now there is no founded evidence as to where the style was first produced. By about 1760, Chippendale was designing in the style of Adam for the various houses that he was working on, and in fact produced some of his best work in the Neo-classical style. He was evidently just as content to work to another's designs as to evolve his own patterns.

Much of the furniture which Adam used as the principal part of his interiors was in fact designed by various firms in the Neo-classical manner, though they were obviously influenced by his ideas. Adam's influence was important in the design of furniture, but his actual style was soon overtaken by Hepplewhite and Sheraton. There are not many pieces that can be dated to his period of fashion, though the effect of his style remained until the close of the century when the Greek revival introduced new fashions and encouraged a fresh study of furniture of the ancient world. The most comprehensive record of Adam's designs can be seen at Sir John Soane's house, now a museum in London, though there is little furniture and most of it was designed to stand against the wall. Adam designed few chairs, the most famous of which can be seen at Osterley House, and most are of carved silver beechwood, with oval backs supported by female sphinxes and have tapered fluted legs. The mahogany chairs of this period have a severity which is completely different from the excessive decoration of their Rococo counterparts. Symmetrical curves and restrained dimensions were the order of the day. Chairs of this design can also be seen at Osterley, particularly one made by John Linnell closely resembling the design of Robert Adam which has a lyre back. These backs were an important decorative contribution to English and continental chair design. The elegant line and feminine quality of the chairs of the Neo-classical period owed much to the use of the heart- or shield-shape back. Finely carved or inlaid decoration of classical themes such as honeysuckle, draperies, urns, pendant husks and wheat ears form the decorative themes which have an affinity with structural lines. Some chairs were painted and decorated to match the general colour of the rooms such as the Etruscan Room, again at Osterley.

George Hepplewhite

The effect of the ideas and designs of George Hepplewhite during the twenty years between 1770 and 1790 developed the Neo-classical style of Robert Adam into a more domestic style suitable for everyday use. The terms "Hepplewhite" and "Sheraton" are in fact only a description of the styles in furniture design of the last part of the eighteenth century. On looking at many of the best examples of the period it can be seen that they bear only a slight likeness to the illustrations in their books. Hepplewhite is associated with the publication of *The Cabinet Maker's and Upholsterer's Guide*, published two years after his death in 1788 by his wife Alice, to whom the business was passed. A second edition appeared in 1789 and a third in 1794. A book of some three hundred designs, it was one of the most useful trade books to be issued in twenty years. As mentioned in his preface, the aims of the guide were "to unite elegance and utility, and blend the useful with the agreeable". It was his aim "to follow the prevailing fashion, omitting such articles as were the production of whim". He disclaimed originality. His name has been associated with shield-back chairs, though he did not introduce them. They do, however, appear frequently in his designs. He was, perhaps, the first to use the Prince of Wales feathers as a chair decoration. Though his designs were copied by other craftsmen, no chair or in fact any piece of furniture can be attributed to his workshop, since he never signed his work and kept no records. In the descriptive notes in the *Guide*, Hepplewhite gives general dimensions of chairs as follows: "Width in front 20″, depth of seat 17″, height of seat

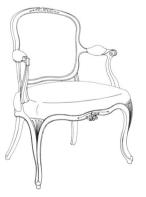

Hepplewhite chair in the French taste. English chairs copied from French originals often have higher front legs than their French counterparts.

26

Two of a set of late-eighteenth-century mahogany dining chairs with turned legs and reeded backs.

Early-nineteenth-century mahogany arm chair with drop-in seat.

frame 17″, total height 3′ 1″″. Legs were square or cylindrical and occasionally a slim curved French-style cabriole, the former terminating in a spade foot. They all tapered, but straight legs tapered only on the inside. The back filling could be a carved in a splat or a specific design—the lyre splat, the wheat ear motif, classical draperies and, of course, the Prince of Wales feathers. Decoration followed the classical theme, medallions, chains of flowers, etc. Whether carved or moulded, the ornament was delicate and refined. Hepplewhite was the first to adopt new forms of decoration, one of them being the new and very elegant fashion for japanning. Chairs were japanned or painted to harmonise with the colour scheme of the room and had a lighter frame-work of beech wood. These types had cane seats with cushions covered with linen or cotton cases to accord with the general hue of the chair. Strong and serviceable chairs were made for dining-rooms and had seats stuffed with horsehair and upholstered with plain striped, chequered material, etc. The third edition of the *Guide* shows a return to square backs for chairs often made of mahogany, and seats of red or blue Morocco leather were recommended. Backs that incorporated medallions of painted or printed silk were inserted in the middle of the top rail. Other seats included in the *Guide* were settees with upholstered backs or of chair back form, hall chairs, wing chairs and the *Duchesse* and *Confidante* chairs. The Duchesse was in fact a composite piece of two facing bergères, or round-backed easy chairs, with a stool between them. The arms of chairs and sofas curved in one smooth line from the back uprights to the front seat, instead of the arm rest supported by

27

Early-nineteenth-century mahogany arm chair with drop-in seat.

A pair of Regency simulated rosewood armchairs.

a short upright rising from the front seat frame.

Some of the chairs of this period are the most graceful and elegant ever made.

Sheraton

Norfolk or Suffolk Sheraton period chair.

Simplicity was the theme of interior decoration during the last years of the eighteenth century, and the furniture of Thomas Sheraton exemplifies this feeling. His book *The Cabinet Maker's and Upholsterer's Drawing Book*, published between 1791 and 1794, showed a wide range of inventive ideas, though he admitted to copying some of the styles fashionable at the time. In many of his designs the style of Louis XVI predominates—a style of extreme elegance and refinement. From the detailed notes of explanation to craftsmen, it is apparent that he had imagination and technical knowledge. Born in Stockton-on-Tees, he arrived in London in 1790 and established himself as a drawing master, making designs for the trade, and publishing books, of which *The Drawing Book* is the most famous. There was also *The Cabinet Dictionary*, 1803, and *The "Unfinished" Encyclopedia*. It is interesting that in *The Cabinet Dictionary*, besides its useful information, appeared some of the first indications of the Regency style that was to follow. Many pieces survive based on his designs, and from these it is very clear that they were widely influential. There is no proof that he ever had a cabinet-making business of his own, or ever made any chairs. In *The Drawing Book* chairs have a feminine lightness and are rather upright,

Two of a set of rare Regency black decorated dining chairs with simulated bamboo splats.

Regency painted beechwood chair. 1800

after nearly a century of curved furniture. Sheraton revived the straight line. The square back is used with straight horizontal top and bottom rails for parlour and dining-room chairs. Vertical lines are emphasised by different and imaginative uses of bars combined into a central splat and decorated with classical motifs. Surviving examples of japanned chairs, usually made of beech, are decorated in black or colour and differ little in design from the mahogany ones. A refinement promoted by Sheraton was that of caning which had been revived and was often used for the seats and backs of chairs. Its use gave a lightness and grace. Chairs for the drawing-room had round fronted seats and were often painted in white and gold. All legs taper and were slender, and often cylindrical, and an additional decoration was reeding. Arms had an upward sweep and met the back near the top, and returned to scroll over the upright from the seat to support the arm rests. Few chairs at this time were made of satin wood, although it is associated with Sheraton.

Chairs of the late eighteenth century show a combination of severity and smoothness of line and proportion.

The Regency Period

Whatever the political or historical facts, the style in furniture during the period between 1800 to 1830 is known as the Regency Period, although it overlaps the political Regency in England 1811 to 1820. Soon after the start of the war with France in 1793, a revolution in taste occurred based on a closer study of

Regency dining-room chair.
1870

English bergère chair.
Early nineteenth century

furniture of the Ancient World—Egypt, Rome and Greece—
and attempts were made to imitate it closely. These ideas became
fashionable at the end of the eighteenth century, and owed much
of their inspiration to the French Directoire style and Greco–
Roman style which was to become the Empire style in France
and in England the Regency style.

It was Henry Holland, 1746 to 1806, a gifted architect who
used furniture of this style when he rebuilt Southill in Bedford-
shire for Samuel Whitbread, in 1795 and enlarged Carlton House
for the Prince of Wales. The main phase of Regency taste stems
from a book published in 1807 *Household Furniture and Interior
Decoration* by Thomas Hope (1770 to 1831), a rich scholar and
traveller who collected antiquities and made drawings of ancient
remains on his extensive travels in Greece, Turkey, Syria and
Egypt. His book illustrated furniture for his own home where he
skilfully adapted designs of furniture of the ancient world.
Hope was followed by George Smith, whose book *A Collection
of Designs for Household Furniture and Decoration* was published
in 1808; this was a comprehensive pattern book in which the
Regency style was brought more into line for the general public
and trade. He adapted ideas from the French and from Sheraton
and Hope. The fashion for Egyptian themes was in vogue
before 1810 and owed much to the publication of D. V. Denon's
Voyage Dans La Basse et Haute Egypte, published in 1804.
Egyptian motifs were incorporated into legs and into the designs
of chairs and other furniture. The sphinx, lotus leaf and lion
supports were in brass inlay. One of the results of the Greek
Revival was the introduction of the Greek *Kismos* chair, which

William IV chair with a cane seat.
1835

William IV rosewood library chairs.
Circa 1835

was skilfully reproduced with well balanced curved uprights at
the back and curved front legs. Bringing about an almost
revolutionary change in chair design based on classical form,
the chair had a broad concave back, but more often it was of
the scroll back form, the uprights scrolling outwards and
backwards to the top. One very elegant version was the parlour
chair which appeared shortly after 1800 and became known as
the *Trafalgar* Chair. It had inward-curving sabre or scimitar
legs usually of oblong form and was narrower at the front than
at the back. A cane seat gave this chair lightness and grace and
was generally covered with a squab cushion. They were often
made of beech wood and painted black or green. Many varieties
are still to be found.

Chairs for the drawing-room were very elaborate, sometimes
of mahogany and sometimes were painted and gilded. During
the early part of the nineteenth century these chairs were
similar to Etruscan style popular in France, which were
inspired by paintings on Greek vases. Strongly curved legs and
scrolled uprights, and arms with a downward sweep were the
main features of these chairs. Thomas Sheraton and George
Smith introduced the use of Monopodia, Lions or Chimera
heads with a single foot, which often formed the arm support
or front legs of chairs. Lion's paws were favoured for feet. The
vogue for the Chinese taste owed much of its inspiration to the
Prince of Wales. The drawing-room at Carlton House contained
some lavishly gilded furniture designed by Holland and executed
with oriental themes. A good deal of black and gold lacquer
furniture was supplied to the Prince Regent at the Brighton

31

Regency chair.
1810

Gothic-style chair in mahogany.
1860

One of a set of six early Victorian
dining chairs. Mahogany with
Gothic backs.

Pavilion. Much japanned furniture was made for the general public, and chairs were often of beech wood, turned and painted to simulate bamboo. The revived taste for Gothic owed much to the romantic novels of Sir Walter Scott whose house, Abbotsford, in Scotland, was built in 1812 in a medieval manner by William Atkinson which affected the architecture of the time. Some chairs were made in the Gothic style and are known as *Abbotsford* chairs. The *Curricle* or *Tub* chair was used in libraries, and the introduction of the French bergère with caned seat and sides gave variety to the type of chair design during this period.

Cabinet makers were beginning to rely on striking effects with grains of some of the new woods being introduced. Rosewood and Zebra wood were widely used, and there was a vogue for Amboyna, Bird's Eye Maple and Coromandel.* Mahogany still remained fashionable for library, dining and bedroom chairs. Brass inlay gained immense popularity and was often incorporated into the backs of chairs. In 1815 the technique for french polishing was introduced; this consisted of shellac dissolved in spirit and applied to carefully prepared surfaces. The result was a brilliant, durable finish to the wood.

The Empire style and its Regency counterpart were the last consistent styles before the industrialism of the nineteenth century engulfed furniture design. From about 1830 all artistic industries were affected in some way by the machine. By 1840 the Industrial and Religious revivals were well under way and the Victorian period had arrived. Comfort was the underlying theme for nineteenth-century chairs. The long reign of Victoria is studded with a variety of styles. There is no tidy sequence

* Imported from South America.

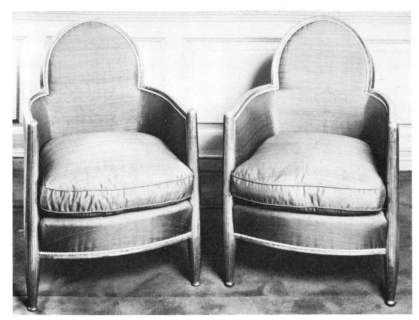

A pair of nineteenth-century Gothic bergère chairs.

Rosewood parlour chair.
1850

as there was in the eighteenth century, and taste gradually began to degenerate in all fields. People in the nineteenth century were living against the background of the Industrial Revolution, and though social conditions were bad for some, amenities had improved. More and more people could afford to buy their own homes and had the money to furnish them. There was the rise of the middle class and greater prosperity for most people.

The first patent coiled spring had been granted in 1828 to Samuel Pratt, a maker of camping equipment in New Bond Street, London, and during the 1830s upholstery changed the proportions of the easy chair. Legs were shortened and the deep seat inclined back and encouraged the habit of "lounging". Upholstery hid much of the frame-work and the seat lost a lot of the elegance of former times. Chairs in the early part of the reign were similar in design to Regency chairs; many other styles that were in fashion then were still in vogue, as many of the pattern books of the Victorian era show. J. C. Louden, in his *Encyclopaedia of Cottage, Farm and Villa Architecture and Furniture*, published in 1833, gives four styles—Greek, Louis XIV, Gothic and Elizabethan, and many other books show an overwhelming variety of styles. The early period is noted for fanciful and picturesque romanticism during which furniture was designed to give the illusion of a particular period, often with conflicting results in the décor, of which the Victorians were unaware. The study of art history was in its infancy. The Regency chair slowly became modified, turned legs replaced the elegant curved ones, the back became the focal point for change and the cresting rail gradually became rounded off to form the

Balloon-back bedroom chair in walnut.
Mid-nineteenth century

Carved walnut drawing-room chair (modern upholstery).
1850

Papier-mâché chair.
1850

Walnut chair with straw seat.

balloon back. In France the revival of the Bourbon monarchy brought an interest in French seventeenth- and eighteenth-century furniture. Given the name of "Old French", it was a concoction of both styles, though mainly Rococo. Often, chairs constructed in this fashion were painted and gilded, and found great popularity in ladies' boudoirs.

The Gothic style owes much to the remarkable genius of Augustus Welby Pugin, 1812 to 1852, who published *True Principles of Pointed or Christian Architecture*. This style developed as a reaction to the light-heartedness that had gone before and was therefore a development of the high moral tone of the time. He designed amounts of Gothic furniture for the newly built Houses of Parliament and Scarisbrick Hall, Lancashire, and his influence was far reaching.

Chairs in the Gothic style were usually made of oak. The *Balloon Back Chair* came into fashion early in the reign, and continued to be produced for many years though by the end of the reign its tremendous popularity was waning. If any chair can be called typically Victorian, it is this one. A change in the character of the curve came about with the search for comfort and resulted in the Balloon Back chair. In the 1830s the cresting rail of the Grecian type was rounded off and gradually evolved into this shape. By about the mid-century the balloon shape was complete, with both cabriole and straight legs. Those with cabriole legs had curved frames, while straight-legged models had, of course, straight frames. They were made out of mahogany and rosewood, and are one of the most comfortable straight chairs to be found. The oval curve of the back fits the

Mid-Victorian slope-frame button-back lady's chair.

Pair of button-back boudoir chairs. 1840

shoulders and the cross rail supports the spine. This style is a great deal more simple than some of the more ornate Victorian furniture. The chairs mix with most furnishings and look well in a modern setting.

The Button-back Chair and Easy Chair have the upholstery fixed with buttons sunk into the thick padding which gives emphasis to the comfort so much loved by the Victorians. There are many examples to choose from, particularly the low-seated easy chairs with or without arms, often with short cabriole legs. The backs are upholstered and spoon shaped. (The chairs without arms have a wooden frame around the curved back outline.) These chairs are still relatively cheap to buy and look very elegant in a bedroom or drawing-room.

The *Prie Dieu Chair*, also known as the *Vesper Chair*, had a tall upholstered back, low seat with short legs, often with turned uprights in the style of the late Stuart period. They were sometimes upholstered with Berlin wool work or Bead work. The Great Exhibition of 1851 at the Crystal Palace, organised by Prince Albert, was the first of its kind, and gave a clear understanding of the tendencies and characteristics of Victorian style. A glance at the catalogue indicates the effect gained by mixing various styles from different countries and also the effect the love and novelty and new materials had on the design of furniture. A predilection for elaborate carving is apparent, and plain surfaces were abhorred (evident in Victorian interiors where everything was crammed together). Invention and the advancement of technical and scientific skill were the things that delighted the Victorians. The machine-carved ornament had

Early Victorian rocking chair in leather.

Victorian bobbin-turned arm chair. 1850

many admirers and there was a fascination in new materials. Beds and chairs were made out of brass and iron. Tubular metal furniture was introduced by Kitschelt of Vienna, and many chairs were designed on the principle that was to be adopted by Marcel Breuer and Le Corbusier at a later date. The purpose of the Great Exhibition, as expressed by Prince Albert, was to present a living picture of the point of development at which mankind had arrived.

The Victorians delighted in experimenting with new materials and there was a great vogue for chairs made in papier mâché, Jennens and Betteridge of Birmingham being the chief manufacturers of this particular material. It was made on a framework of wood, or even metal, and a smooth surface was japanned in black. It was then painted with flowers and gilded, or had a mother-of-pearl inlay.

A successful innovation in chair design started by Michael Thonet was the *Bentwood Chair*, which was structurally simple and easy to manufacture. Using steam power he bent beechwood to the required shape and used cane work and plywood for the seats. Ahead of his time in his production methods, Thonet exhibited at the Great Exhibition. From then onwards his chairs found favour for their lightness and grace in hotels, shops, restaurants and public buildings, and are still produced today. The Thonet rocking chair is very popular.

It was William Morris who, after the Great Exhibition, was to show his disapproval of industrial design. He set about trying to improve the applied arts of the day, and founded the firm of Morris & Company in 1861 with some friends. It was

Late-nineteenth-century beech and
oak turned chair with a caned seat.
1880

Early Victorian settee.

Morris's taste for the simple and straightforward that inspired
the designers that were to follow him. If Morris decoration looks
to us today Victorian, with its medieval feeling, we must
try to remember that it was Morris's ideals that guided it rather
than his taste, and he inspired his craftsmen to take a pride in
their work. The effect on chair design was to produce simple
chairs, in particular one based on a traditional Sussex Chair
which had a rush seat, simple turned legs and was stained black.
The other most famous of Morris chairs was the adjustable
chair, made in about 1866. It had a long seat and an adjustable
back, and was popular not only in England, but in the United
States, where at this time English furniture was enjoying a
particular vogue due mostly to the publication of Charlelock
Eastlake's book, *Hints on Household Taste*, published in 1868.
The furniture he favoured was vaguely traditional, based on
early English styles.

In the last two decades of the century there developed a style
known as Art Furniture. Produced by such firms as Heal's,
Liberty and Morris & Company, the aim was to provide furniture with an aesthetic appeal, and to achieve this they used the
talents of established architects, artists and designers such as
Christopher Dresser, Bruce Talbert, William Burgess, Phillip
Webb and John Chapple.

The taste for Japanese art was felt after the Americans had
opened up Japan to the rest of the world in 1859. W. E. W.
Godwin, an architect, who was one of the first people to take an
interest in the particular style, was inspired to design light and
elegant chairs in a manner ahead of their time. Naturally, as in

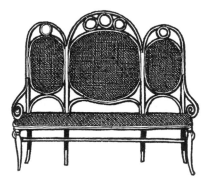

Thonet Bentwood settee.

Adjustable chair in William Morris's style.
1880

A pair of chairs designed by Gaillard.
1900

every field of design, the style degenerated with mass production and chairs were produced in flimsy bamboo. Another architect to have some influence at this time was T. E. Colcutt, 1840 to 1924, who designed furniture and chairs with simple lines. Due to the inspiration of William Morris many movements were formed after 1880 with the influence of the Arts and Crafts movement. A. A. Mackmurdo formed The Century Guild in 1882. This was the first of many such societies of craftsmen formed to produce well-designed furniture, though it was not all simple as in the Morris style, but was often inspired by lines of the early eighteenth century. All were overshadowed by the growing Art Nouveau Movement.

Charles II arm chair in walnut
upholstered in velvet, one of a pair.
About 1670

Chapter 2
French Chairs

Historical Background

The history of French furniture goes back much farther than that of English. Continental craftsmen were more advanced in skill and technique than their English counterparts and have therefore left more to posterity.

Life in fourteenth- and fifteenth-century France was grim and austere. The people, including artists and craftsmen, were gripped in a period of religious fervour, and this was reflected in furniture styles. All furniture at this time was made out of oak. The most prevalent piece of furniture of the early Gothic period was the chest, which served as a seat as well as storage place and as a trunk for the owner when he moved; life in the middle ages was politically and socially unstable and at the slightest warning whole households would be on the move.

The throne chair is really a chest with added back and sides. It is derived from the chest as its base is in itself a chest, often fitted with a lock, and decorated with Gothic tracery but was often draped with hangings and cushions called *carreaux* which hid the seat. The back decoration commenced at a point level with the sitter's head, leaving the lowest panel which served as a back rest bare (this was the only part with any decoration). This particular chair was used for important occasions with material draped over it and was placed against the wall. The reverse side was left undecorated. The bench, in use from earlier times, continued to be used.

By the end of the fifteenth century the influence of the Italian Renaissance was noticeable in France. It had been almost a

Papier-mâché chair, painted and inlaid with gilt and mother of pearl. 1850

39

Throne chair in oak with lion finials, rising seat and scratched decoration. Fifteenth century

High Gothic throne chair (seat not original). Cresting intact, book fold panelling on front and sides. Late fifteenth century

French Renaissance arm chair in walnut with architectural features.

century since the Italians had abandoned Gothic tradition and had gone in search of new forms of design based on the Classical world. Many of these ideas reached France after 1495 when Charles VIII invaded Italy. The invading French came upon a new world of culture undreamed of in Gothic France, and not only did Charles VIII return with a rich booty but he also brought back craftsmen from Italy to assist with the building and decorating of his castle of Amboise in the Loire valley. Thus began the first influence of the Italian Renaissance in France.

The reign of Francis I, son of Charles VIII, ushered in the French Renaissance. He succeeded to the throne of Louis XII in 1515 and moved the French court from the Loire valley, where it had been established for over one hundred years, to Fontainebleau, where he tried to imitate the patronage and courtly life of the Italian Princes. The architects, painters, sculptors and furniture makers employed at Fontainebleau, many of whom were Italian, borrowed their decorations and ideas from the Italian Renaissance. Their work, in what became known as the "School of Fontainebleau" had a far-reaching effect on French art that followed, although, of course interpretations by individuals varied.

It is often difficult to distinguish the furniture of the Francis I period from Italian pieces of the same time, as both utilised the same leaf motifs, busts, and pilasters decorated with arabesques and grotesques. Chairs of this period often retained their Gothic form but incorporated many Renaissance features. One used very commonly was the medallion, designed as a head in profile

One of a pair of fine Louis XIII walnut arm chairs, upholstered in tapestry. Turned square legs joined by similar stretchers.

French walnut chairs with bobbin and reel turning. Mid-seventeenth century (tapestry covers later seventeenth century)

or full face and wreathed in foliage. The ornament known as *Grotesques* was inspired by the Loggia Frescoes by Raphael in the Vatican. These were in great demand and appeared often on the chairs of the time. With any change in social life, seat furniture is often one of the first pieces of furniture to show it. In the Middle Ages there were two state chairs—the *Foldstool* and the *Throne*. The metal foldstool disappeared by the early sixteenth century but its shape was retained in many of the chairs of the period. *Pincer Chairs*, folding chairs and folding stools were all in use but were made of oak instead of metal. The Throne was still used by important personages, but was decorated with Renaissance motifs.

Henry II Style (1547 to 1589)

During this period furniture was modified structurally and brought more into line with Italian Renaissance principles. A very definite and beautiful style evolved at Fontainebleau; in fact, seat furniture grew much lighter, chairs gradually developed into more portable types, the arms being freed by the removals of the sides. Mention is made of the name "chaise à bras"—the early French word for arm chair. The seat, instead of being a chest (or box) was freed by the removal of the panels, leaving only the frame. The back gradually became lower and appeared in splat back form. Legs took the shape of columns, tapering slightly at the top and bottom and having a base and moulding suggesting a base and capital. They were joined near the floor with stretchers which were put together in a rectangular frame. Seats were usually made of wood on a square plan. There are many examples in continental museums—one type in particular is the *Caquetoire* which had a trapezoid seat resting on four legs or on a single pivot.

Jacques Androuet, known as Du Cerceau (1515 to 1554), was an architect and draughtsman who had studied under Dorato Bramante in Italy. His publication *Gravé de Meubles* (1550) brought about an aesthetic approach to furniture making which was inspired by the antique, not only in decoration but in rules of proportion and in choice of form.

The School of Burgundy was greatly influenced by art of the low countries. Hugues Sambin, an architect, sculptor and cabinet maker worked in Dijon (1549 to 1572) and his work is a good example of this school. Sambin's furniture was characterised by the use of bold human figures and by the surface covered completely with carving. Regional styles merged and a single style evolved throughout France. Walnut, a soft and easily carved wood, lent itself well to this sculptural style. However, furniture was scarce at the time, even for the rich nobles. The woven fabrics and furnishings in use were a great feature of this period. Rich and beautiful fabrics were scattered over beds, chairs and tables. Square cushions were placed on seats. This lack of furniture was perhaps due to the civil and religious wars that split and drained the country between 1562 and 1598.

Henry IV (1589 to 1610)

Henry IV established foreign craftsmen in 1608 in the Louvre. Many were Flemish, as he wished to make France self-sufficient and not dependent on foreign states for luxury items. The presence of foreign craftsmen in the Louvre stimulated the native wood workers, introducing them to the up-to-date styles from Italy and Flanders.

Louis XIII (1610 to 1643)

With the death of Henry IV in 1610 the country fell into the hands of the Queen Regent, Marie de Medici, a Florentine, but a devotee of Flemish art. She was followed as Regent by Anne of Austria, the wife of Louis XIII (who was Spanish), who was greatly under the influence of Cardinal Mazarin, an Italian. It is during this period that two names are given for the title of "chair". *Fauteuils* (arm chairs) now had arm rests and broad backs. Louis XIII arm chairs had hard, straight backs, often of greater width than height.

Legs were usually turned and linked by cross stretchers and the front legs were joined by an extra stretcher carved and decorated with coats of arms. The arm supports were an exten-

Louis XIV arm chair with waved stretchers.

Arm chair from rare suite of Louis XIV walnut seat furniture.

Louis XIV fauteuil in walnut. 1680

sion of the legs; arm rests were straight and terminated in female busts or lions' heads.

The name *Chaise* (chair) was now used when referring to a chair without arm rests, and the style is similar to the arm chair. The fashion for the farthingale brought about the *Chaise à Vertugadin* which enabled the ladies to sit with ease (which would have been impossible in an arm chair). The backs of these chairs incorporated a foliated motif and the seat was trapezoid. It rested on four legs slanting outwards to the ground. This style of chair remained in vogue only while the fashion for farthingales remained.

The first real upholstery of chairs began in this period. The carreaux were discarded and were replaced by fixed upholstery which was nailed straight on to the frame-work. Under this went horsehair covered with rough material, making a base for the upholstery, which included embossed leathers, either gilt or painted *à la Mauresque*, or fabric. Wool upholstery fabrics were much in use during the reign of Henry II, Henry IV and Louis XIII. These were called *moquettes* in France and in Europe *Velours d'Utrecht* (the earliest place to manufacture them). While their texture and design differed from the French material, they were similar in appearance. The earlier French moquette is of small design and in many colours. The Velours was usually one tone with a large stamped pattern. The upholstery was attached to the chair with brass and silver studs and nails which counterbalance the sober and massive character of this type of seat furniture. These chairs are represented so well in the engravings of Abraham Bosse (1602 to 1672) which can be seen

One of a pair of Régence polished beechwood fauteuils each with a nailed, calf-covered shaped back and serpentine-fronted seat, the frame of the back carved with an asymmetrical flame moulding at the centre and with leaf clasps at the side, the arms with husks and leaves joining the shell handles. Cabriole legs headed by acanthus leaves joined by moulded "X"-shaped stretchers and the centre of the seat rail carved with asymmetrical Rococo mouldings.
Circa 1740

Provincial walnut wing arm chair. 1740

One of a pair of fine Régence tapestry-covered walnut fauteuils with rectangular seats and arched backs covered in contemporary tapestry.

in the Victoria and Albert Museum in London and in many French museums.

Louis XIV (1661 to 1715)

The introduction of foreign furniture and a more luxurious way of life owed much to the two Cardinals Richelieu and Mazarin. Mazarin, an Italian, surrounded himself with luxury unequalled in France, as can be seen in the inventory of his possessions drawn up after his death which is in the Archives de Condé (Inventaire de tous les Meubles du Cardinal Mazarin dressé en 1653 et publié d'apres l'originale). He acquired many pieces from other countries but many were made by foreign craftsmen working in France who were to play a leading part in the development of the Louis XIV style after Mazarin's death in 1661. However, they were not always greeted with enthusiasm by French craftsmen.

By 1657 Nicholas Fouquet, Mazarin's Finance Minister, was starting to build Vaux le Vicomte ("ce Versailles anticipe", states Sainte-Beuve), and had assembled a considerable number of French craftsmen to assist with the building. With the arrest of Fouquet in 1659 the King took over the tapestry works at Maincy which was the centre to which all the craftsmen working at Vaux were attached, retaining some of Fouquet's workmen for his own employment there. In 1667 he took a decision that was to have a profound effect on the decorative arts in France and transferred the tapestry works from Maincy to the old-

Louis XV gilt wood end section to a chaise-longue.

Louis XV painted fauteuil de bureau, the shaped and nailed leather-covered back with a moulded frame carved with sprays of flowers, the serpentine-fronted revolving seat with a loose cushion, the moulded seat rail carved with leaves and with cabriole legs and painted in blue-green on a chalk-grey ground.

established workshops of the Gobelin family in Paris and establishing the *Manufature Royale des Meubles de la Courounne*. The formation of this centralised organisation for the manufacture of luxury arts owed much to Jean Baptiste Colbert, Louis XIV's Finance Minister. But without the able guidance of Charles le Brun (1619 to 1690), *Premier Peintre du Roi* (who had worked for Fouquet at Vaux) the work at the Gobelin factory would have been rather staid. Le Brun was able to impose a unity of style and form on all that was made there for the royal Palaces. The King and Colbert established the *Manufature des Gobelins* with two purposes in mind—one to provide furnishings of a certain standard for the royal Palaces, the other to raise the standard of luxury arts in France.

After drawing on foreign ideas for nearly two centuries, a true French style evolved around 1660. After the mid-seventeenth century it was France that the rest of Europe looked to for cultural inspiration and stimulus. The King played the main part in this evolution and from 1661 created around himself, at Versailles, a setting that was rich and sumptuous, one that would heighten the prestige of the court in the eyes of the rest of Europe. Life at Versailles was formal, governed by the strictest protocol, and this is reflected in the furniture of that time.

Early Louis XV gilt wood canapé with a rectangular, slightly arched, stuffed back of scrolled outline interspersed with sprays of marguerites and leaves, curved wings and inswept moulded arm supports. Seat rail centred by marguerites and sprays of leaves and raised on cabriole legs with leaf-capped feet. Six feet, eight inches long.

Louis XV walnut chair. 1754

Furniture

During the reign of Louis XIV, furniture and decoration took on a magnificent and regal style. Chairs of the period mirror the feeling for greatness—they are heavy and massive and appear very ornate with all the feeling of magnificence. The upholstered arm chair had a feeling of strength and immobility and, in fact, needed several people to move a single one. The high raked back seems designed to frame the elaborated wigs worn at the time. The arm chairs had a high rectangular upholstered back with no wood showing. The arm rests are of wood, usually walnut, and are deeply curved, ending in large scrolls, often acanthus leaves. Arm pads came into use at the end of the century. The seat is usually square in shape, legs are carved or moulded, tapering or baluster, or square sections with fluted pedestals capped by mouldings with mushroom-shaped profiles. The heaviness of the chairs gave rise to either the "H"- or "X"-shaped stretchers. The centre of the "X"-shaped stretcher was a pretext for an elaborately carved motif. Most chairs were made of walnut, which was carved and polished. The more elaborate carved, gessoed and gilded chairs were usually of oak.

For the modest household, chairs were made by copying the general lines of the grander ones, lacking the extravagant carving and gilding but retaining the strong heavy mouldings which were a feature of all chairs of the period. These simpler chairs have plain legs and stretchers—arms were a copy of the Volute and were given the name *Chaise à bec de corbin* in some parts of France, because of the resemblance to a crow's beak.

A pair of rare Régence walnut single chairs with carved backs. *Circa* 1720

Louis XV bergère chair in carved beechwood by P. Bernard. *Circa* 1765

Towards the end of the seventeenth century the cabriole leg made its appearance. Its origin was to be found in Chinese furniture and it was used frequently in fashionable chair design, terminating in a *pied de biche*. It was to remain in fashion for over sixty years. The fashion for upholstered furniture continued as in the previous reign of Louis XIII. The *Confessional* or *Fauteuil de Commodité* appeared, with a high back which has oreilles (ears or wings) on each side for resting the head. The seat was detachable and was fitted with a square cushion. It was a chair in which the sitter could relax, very different from the seating at court where etiquette ruled the day. The importance of the stool in court life led to many rivalries. There were two types of stool—the *Tabouret* or fixed stool, on which only the noblest could sit, and the *Ployant* or folding stool for less important people. Only the King was allowed to sit on an arm chair at court, though chairs without arms were in general use outside the court. Saint-Simon's *Memoirs* bring home the important part the stool played in Court etiquette. "Le fauteuil à bras, la chaise à dos, le tabouret, on été pendant plusieurs siècles des importants objets de politique et d'illustres sujets de querelles."

Towards the mid-century the *Canapé* (or Canopé) settee evolving from the *lit de répos* appeared. It was not unlike a large arm chair, six or eight feet wide so that several people could sit on it at the same time. Sets of arm chairs were made to match the canapé.

A light and easily moved chair that evolved at the end of the century was the *Chauffeuse*. It had a low upholstered seat and

47

Louis XV walnut chaise-longue in three parts. Six feet, eleven inches long.

Louis XV beechwood and walnut bergère, the arched and moulded back carved at the centre with a spray of flowers, with out-curved and moulded arm facings.

could be used to sit close to the fire and for nursing children. One of the most charming chairs appeared about the same time— the *Chaise à capucine*, a small chair with turned legs and horizontal slats shaped like a simplified scroll. It found a place in both the greatest and simplest homes and even at court where silk cushions were tied to its straw seat. It became everybody's chair in the eighteenth century and is often shown in the interiors of such genre painters as Chardin and Greuze. An innovation to upholstery evolved during the reign of Louis XIV. The fauteuil or canapé chassis was devised in which upholstery fabric covered a wooden frame-work which slipped into the frame of the chair. This idea made it possible to change the decoration of the room according to the seasons. Heavily embroidered fabrics were used in the winter and lighter colours and material in the spring and summer.

After the King's morganatic marriage to the Marquise de Maintenon, court life at Versailles became less formal and there was a tendency to unbend towards greater ease and comfort. This change in social conditions can be studied step by step through the construction of chairs made during the transition. Even before the end of his reign new ideas and designs were affecting decoration and ornament. The sculptor, engraver and designer Jean Berain, as well as Paul le Pautre, had begun to introduce whimsical designs with delicate arabesques and carvings of birds and leaves in low relief. Monkeys playing the part of humans were also introduced at this time. This form of decoration was used on the wall panels and cornices, replacing the heavy classical style. This Rococo style was well established

An eighteenth-century beechwood stool with cabriole legs. One of a pair of Louis XV waxed beechwood chairs signed "Nagaret à Lyon".

A Louis XVI provincial bergère chair. 1765

before the death of Louis XIV in 1715.

Régence

After the death of Louis XIV the court at Versailles ceased to be the centre of social life. Louis XV was only five years old, making it necessary to appoint a Regent. From 1715 to 1723 Philippe II, Duc d'Orleans was Regent of France. In cabinet work the Régence period extends from 1700 to 1720, and during this period there was to develop a most imaginative style known as Rococo or Rocaille. It differed from Baroque in its lightness and lack of restrained symmetry, but by 1750 it had become subdued and restrained in the perfected style of Louis XV.

For the first time in its existence Versailles was without a King and there was a break in the extravagant court grandeur that had been such an essential feature of life there. The high expenditure had left its mark on the country's finances and as a result the aristocracy had either to live in a quieter manner or to seek a new source of income. Many members of the nobility contracted marriages with humbler but wealthier classes —merchants and bankers. An increasingly rich bourgeoisie were building themselves large hôtels in Paris and many of the nobles made Paris the centre of social life, the Regent among them at the Palais Royale. The grandeur of the Salon gave way to fashion for the small boudoir and furniture became smaller in scale and elegance to fit the less lofty surroundings. The

Large Canapé, part of a large suite of Louis XVI seat furniture.

A large Louis XVI painted
arm chair with oval back and carved,
fluted legs, covered in Aubusson
tapestry.
Circa 1780

Régence style has no real valid existence. Like the Directoire
style it is a convenient term for furniture still retaining features
of Louis XIV but displaying some that belong to the Louis XV
style.

The chairs of this time give a complete picture of the transition
from the formal Louis XIV style to the Louis XV. The formal
arm chair of the Louis XIV period was gradually replaced and
small differences began to appear. The first of these was that
the arms, which before had risen directly over the legs, were
placed much farther back and the legs reduced in height,
allowing for greater ease and comfort. This new position for
the arms has been attributed to the fashion for panniers for the
ladies' dresses at the time. The legs were also slightly curved
and elaborately carved as was the woodwork of the frame. The
seat was now on show instead of being covered by upholstery,
and chairs usually had arm pads. The shell was used a good
deal as a decorative motif. Legs ended in a cloven hoof, the
height of the backs was reduced and a gentle curve appeared
in place of the rectangular lines of the previous period. Instead
of being covered the wood around the back frame was now
visible. The curves of the legs increased and the feet ended in
scrolls under which small bases were carved. The "X"-shaped
stretchers, so prevalent during Louis XIV's reign, disappeared,
and a chair evolved that had not a straight line.

Fauteuil from a set of Louis XVI painted seat furniture comprising a canapé, a pair of fauteuils and four single chairs. Grey-painted frames with gilt mouldings.

Pair of Louis XVI arm chairs with oval carved backs, upholstered in tapestry.

Themes of Rococo or Rocaille

The Rocaille or Rococo style with its intricate asymmetrical forms evolved from the baroque during the Régence period and was used by French craftsmen from 1720 to about 1755 to 1760. The term was not used during the reign of Louis XV. Rocaille, meaning rock work, was used not to describe asymmetrical ornament but for the fascinating artificial grottoes which were fashionable in Italian and French gardens during the Renaissance. Rocailles were usually decorated with natural rocks encrusted with pebbles and shells and often shaped to look like waterfalls, crests of waves and other ornaments. These ornaments were modified by ornamentists such as Nicholas Pineau (1684 to 1754) and Claude Audran III (1688 to 1734), who was a disciple of Berain. The word *rocaille* was used to indicate a fashion in decoration and dates from the end of the eighteenth century. The term Rococo occurred much later. The theme was "Imagination", using rocks and shells with flowers and foliage as the main features, asymmetry and contrast playing a great part. Gilles Marie Oppenord (1672 to 1742) and Juste Aurèle Meissonier (1693 to 1750) were perhaps the two main designers to use this form of decoration and around 1730 great use of contorted natural forms was to be found. Pineau, Jacques de Lajoue (born in 1686) and Meissonier are sometimes thought to be the main creators of this earlier phase. By about 1750 the style had been modified and had become the perfected Louis XV style. Using moderately curved lines it was, in fact, Rocaille in a restrained form.

51

Louis XV Marquise by Louis Delanois.

One of a pair of Louis XV waxed beechwood chairs signed "Nagaret à Lyon".

The Louis XV style is perhaps the most characteristically French of all styles. It has a lightened elegance and one of the main features that French artists had assimilated was asymmetry which was to remain in vogue until the Classical revival.

Louis XV Style

This style neither began nor ended with the reign of the King. Michelet the French historian wrote in his *Histoire de France du XVIème Siècle* "It was a return to the sense of life and humanity", a statement that fits the period exactly.

The interior of the Louis XV style house underwent a change, perhaps due to the desire for more comfort and domestic privacy and with an eye to the amenities required for the social life of the time. Rooms were reduced in scale to become more suited to human needs. During the reign of Louis XIV interiors had consisted of long suites of connecting rooms decorated in a grand manner in which all practicality was sacrificed to magnificence. Often these rooms were comfortless, but by the eighteenth century this had changed and the architect was able to put twice as many rooms into the same space. Each had its special character and use, such as the large drawing-room, little rooms or cabinets for music or reading, or the self-explanatory *cabinet de café* and the *cabinet de lecture*. The rooms were decorated with wood panelling, painted and gilded and often framed with delicate mouldings, relieved by painted papers from China and India. Walls were often hung with the same

Two of a set of three Louis XV painted chairs stamped "I. Gourdin" including a fauteuil. Jean-Baptiste Gourdin, whose father and younger brother were also menuisiers, was received Master in 1748 and worked up to 1776.

material as used for chair upholstery and curtains. Furniture became smaller and more suited for comfort. It was also easier to move. An apt description of the Louis XV style of furniture would be that it was suited to human needs, the needs of all spheres of society. The modest pieces made for townspeople often have more beauty of line than the more ambitious items. The real beauty of this furniture is the smooth supple lines and not its rich decoration. There is a great harmony in the combination of graceful and delicate mouldings. Straight lines were avoided and only used when absolutely necessary. In the chairs of Louis XV there is not a straight line to be seen. Many chairs have no decoration and rely solely on the delicate mouldings and gentle swelling curve for their aesthetic value. Asymmetry is a feature on Louis XV furniture and the French craftsmen were able to achieve this without losing the balance of a piece.

Furniture makers during the reign of Louis XV took delight in creating new forms in furniture to suit a society given to the pursuit of pleasure—a society dedicated to material comforts. The chairs of the period appear to be moulded to fit the shape of the sitter, having seats with concave curved backs called *cabriolet*. Seats were made low as if to invite a more relaxed posture. They were eighteen to twenty inches wide in the reign of Louis XIV but those of Louis XV were only about fourteen to sixteen inches wide. Most chairs were made of beech but some menuisiers made use of walnut, lime and cherry. In the provincial districts fruit wood was popular and menuisiers used cherry, pear, chestnut and olive. Menuisiers went to great pains

A pair of Louis XV needlework-covered painted fauteuils stamped "Tilliard". Cartouche-shaped backs and serpentine-fronted seats covered, as are the arm pads, in a silk gros point. The cabriole legs with scrolls at the knees and leaf sabots. (Jena-Baptiste Tilliard I, who died in 1764, and his son who took over the business when his father died, both used the same stamp.)

to design chairs for every conceivable use, but one theme runs through these chairs. They are all gracefully curved in a continuous line from the back to the foot, the moulding on the legs runs to the valence without a break, and the arm and leg seem to be made out of one single piece of wood, the lack of straight lines being one of the main features of Louis XV furniture.

Chairs may be divided into two distinct types—the *siège à la Reine*, a tribute to Marie Lescznska, the wife of Louis XV, with a flat back, and the *siège en Cabriolet*, where the back is concave. The back of the Louis XV chair is much lower than that of the Régence arm chair. It was no higher than the height of the shoulders of the sitter. Legs are cabriole and stretchers disappear. The Louis XV arm chairs were easily moved and were well suited to the elegant day-to-day life of the period.

Chairs of the Period

The *sièges meublants* had their fixed position along the walls of reception rooms whose designs matched the mouldings of the wall panels and whose carving echoed similar decorative motifs. The *sièges courants* were intended to be moved around the room as needed for card games, conversations, etc.

The *Voyeuse* or *Voyelle* was a conversation chair designed like an ordinary chair or arm chair but having a flat curving top rail which allowed a person to rest his elbows while watching a game of cards. The seat was sometimes designed so that the sitter could sit astride.

Regency child's high chair; the height is adjustable. About 1840

Two beechwood bergère chairs in the manner of Lebas.
Circa 1765

Floral, foliage and shell patterns were carved to decorate the moulded frame-work of the chairs and even the simplest of chairs has a flower carved in the centre of the top rail, on the cabriole legs and on the apron. The *cartouche* back was often favoured for fauteuils. To receive the fashionable panhiers, arm supports were set back and joined into the seat rail. When the arms were not set back on the fauteuils they were placed above the front legs and curved backwards and outwards at the same time. Usually these chairs have a padded elbow rest (a *manchette*). The canapé was made in a variety of styles. The small *marquise* or *casseuse* was rather like an enlarged arm chair and similar to the English love-seat which could seat two. Canapés were usually designed to seat three people. The basket shape was perhaps the most fashionable and it was known as the *ottomane* or *canapé à corbeille*, as the arches and curves of its back formed a half circle. It was usual for cushions to be placed at each end and has a long loose seat cushion for extra comfort.

The names for some of the seat furniture reflect the role woman played in society and emphasise her ascendency. *La Reine*, *en confessional*, *fauteuil de poudrer*, and the forms taken by *chaises-longues* and day beds all underline this point. Few chairs of the eighteenth century will still have their original covering. Silk, satin, velvet and damask were used most often. Tapestry was used occasionally for chairs and sofas, but mostly as wall coverings, and the practise of making them a part of the general decorative scheme was emphasised by sometimes having sofas and chairs covered *en suite*.

Leather covered wing chair.
About 1840

55

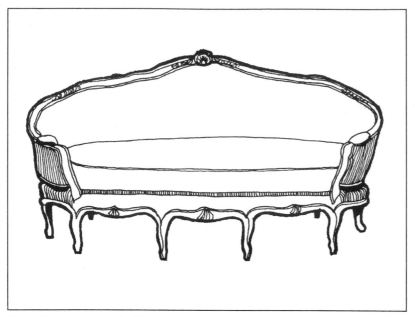

Louis XV canapé à corbeille.

One of a set of twelve chairs and settee signed "G. Jacob".

The day bed was given a variety of names and was made in many shapes, such as the *turquoise*, *sultana*, *veilleuse* and *duchesse*. The duchesse had a gondola-shaped back and was perhaps the most well known. It was fashionable from 1740 to about 1780. The *duchesse brisée* was similar to the duchesse but was designed in three parts having a bergère, a stool with concave sides and a low bergère called a *bout de pied*. The turquoise and sultana reflect the fascination for anything Turkish in this period. The turquoise had two back pieces of equal size, a mattress and two square and two round cushions. The veilleuse was a large ottoman with a sloping back higher at one end, where head rests were placed. The chaise-longue was made up of a bergère with a mattress and deeply upholstered wings like a confessional.

Fauteuils de Cabinet

Chairs designed for the writing table had low round backs. They were sometimes circular and occasionally on a pivot. Occasionally also, they were semi-circular at the back and curved at the front with one convex curve between two concave ones. These chairs have three front legs and a single back leg, and are generally covered in leather. Lighter chairs were made out of cane their shape being the same as that of the upholstered chairs, with frames of varnished or painted cherry, walnut and beech. They were sometimes gilded along with the cane work. During the summer they were left bare and in the winter square cushions were fixed to the seats and backs. Leather was often

One of a pair of rare Louis XVI carved and painted marquises.

One of a pair of fine Louis XVI bergères, painted grey and signed "G. Jacob". Generously proportioned, it has a rectangular back and down-curved arms on inswept moulded supports, capped by acanthus leaves. Moulded seat rails and short tapering legs headed by paterae.

used for the pads on the arms. Toilet chairs were also caned as the powder used for hair and face would have spoiled upholstery, so they were cushioned with leather. The top back rail was dipped to receive the neck whilst the hair was being arranged.

The chairs of this time were designed for comfort and were of a convenient size. No other part of furniture reveals more about this period than do the seats. The large comfortable bergère conveys to the eye the change in domestic habits and it was the last word in comfort. Madame Capan writes in her memoirs how one of Louis XV's daughters, Madame Louise, had become a nun and she feared that Madame Victoire, her sister might follow suit. Madame Victoire looked at a comfortable bergère and replied "Here is a chair that will be my ruin". The bergère appeared in about 1725 and had solid sides with no opening between the arms and seat. A loose cushion gave extra comfort. It was made in many forms of which three are especially well known. One type was rather like the fauteuil but had closed sides, another, perhaps the most familiar, had a rounded shape. The wing chair was a form of bergère. Of confessional shape it had wings or ears-*aux oreilles*.

Coverings

The fabrics which covered the chair seats were as numerous as the types of chairs. For the most expensive seats tapestry was used, mostly made at Beauvais. Themes were bouquets and running

Louis XV fauteuil à coiffer.

Louis XVI grey-painted bergère in the manner of Jacob (the design and quality of the carving suggest that this is the work of Georges Jacob, the attribution being strengthened by the steeply chamfered seat rails much used by him).

bands of flowers, draperies with cords, La Fontaine's fables, pastorales and monkey pieces. At Elbeuf and Rouen a tapestry called *bergame* was produced with designs of stripes and chevrons in graduated tones. A cheaper tapestry in use for covering chairs in ante-rooms was tapestry worked with needle and canvas in fine or coarse stitch or both and usually made by women employed by the lady of the house to do only this. The richest and most durable of silken materials other than velvet was damask which was used for covering seats. There was three-coloured damask and Genoa damask. The most popular colours were green, and crimson. Yellow and blue were not, it appears, so fashionable. On yellow damask the nails had to be of silver. A thick variety of taffeta, *gros de Tours* was reserved for summer furniture. Loose covers were made to slip over tapestry or damask chairs for the summer months. Pekin silk (which, despite its name, was made in France) was hand painted with flowers, and used also in the summer. There was much embroidered satin and plain striped brocade, moiré was less fragile but rather harsh in appearance. Genoa velvet was costly but it looked rich and splendid. The stamped velvet with ribs and stripes was also in great demand. Brocatelle has a satiny ground patterned with freshly coloured flowers and was cheaper but less durable than damask, being a mixture of silk and cotton. For seats which were in constant use and on which these expensive fabrics would have been out of place a covering called *moquette* was used. It was also used for carpets, chair and table covers, hangings, dining-room and library chairs and many more.

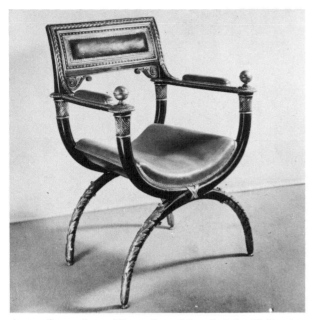

A very fine and rare Directoire writing chair by G. Jacob with gilt enrichments on a dark green ground. *Circa* 1765

Louis XV fauteuil de bureau.

Perhaps the most famous woman of the Rococo age was Madame de Pompadour who, though she did not change the course of French history had a great influence on the decorative arts of the day. Her death is recorded by Louis Petit de Bachaumont in his *Memoires Secrets*. "On April 15th, 1764, this evening, Madame de Pompadour died. The distinguished protection she afforded to men of letters and her taste for the arts make it impossible to pass over this sad event in silence." From 1745 to 1764 she was the mistress of Louis XV. A woman of exquisite taste, she gave her patronage to artists and craftsmen, having many houses to furnish. Chateaux were built or altered for her at Versailles, Fontainebleau, Crécy, Champs, Bellevue and Menars, as well as the Hotel d'Evreux in Paris and suites of apartments at Versailles and Marly. She therefore had to buy a great deal of furniture, and Lazare Duvaux, a Parisian dealer of furniture and curios, recorded in his day book that Madame de Pompadour was his principal customer. Numerous artists were constantly receiving commissions from her. Her favourite painters were perhaps Carle Van Loo (1705 to 1765) and François Boucher (1703 to 1770), two of the most successful exponents of the Rococo style in painting. A good deal has been written about her but it should be recognised that she advised and supported some of the best artists and craftsmen of her day. Through her influence, Madame de Pompadour's brother, the Marquis de Venières (later created the Marquis de Marigny), was given the post of Director of Buildings. From the end of 1749 to 1751 he prepared himself for that position by journeying through Italy with the architect Jacques Germain

Directoire chairs with white and gilt decoration and black hide coverings.

Soufflot and the artist and engraver Nicholas Charles Cochin. In 1758 Cochin published *Antiquities of Herculaneum* which helped to spark off the beginnings of the Neo-classical style.

An undercurrent of protest against the curved line of the Rococo had not ceased since its birth. One of the most scathing attacks came from Cochin in 1754. The discoveries of Herculaneum and Pompeii brought about an overwhelming enthusiasm for the Antique which began around 1750 to 1755. This led from the Louis XV style to the Louis XVI Neo-classical style, which was forming before the accession of the King in 1744. Furniture of this period displays a compromise between Rococo and Classicism.

The Louis XVI Neo-classical Style

The study of classical remains was one which attracted great interest during the eighteenth century. This interest was spurred on by the rediscovery of the buried cities of Herculaneum and Pompeii which excited an interest in the classical world. With the systematic excavation of these two Roman cities people in the eighteenth century were able to gain considerable knowledge of the decorative arts of the Romans. A closer study of the antique brought about numerous publications on ancient Greece and Italy. A series of volumes was published between 1752 and 1767 by the Comte de Caylus and had a widespread influence. It was entitled *Recueil d'antiquités Egyptiennes, Etrusques, Grecques, Romaines et Gauloises*, and brought to the

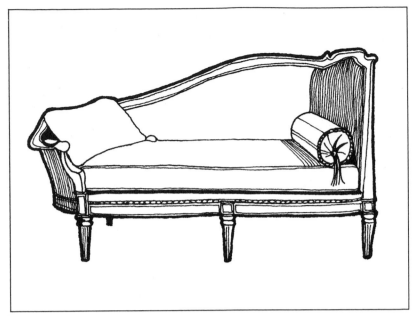

Louis XVI ottoman.

attention of artists and designers a completely new collection
of decorative themes. Abbé Johann Wincklemann's *Geschichte
der Kunst des Altertums*, published in 1764, was more on the
theoretical side and gave advice to artists.

The collective imagination was inspired by a collection of
engravings by the talented Venetian etcher Giovanni Battista
Piranesi (1720 to 1778), whose plates praised the beauties of
imperial Rome. Using the techniques of chiaroscuro he gave
emphasis to the collonades and great ruined arches conveying
a feeling of mystery and romance about the past which gave rise
to poetic and melancholy emotions for all who saw them. An
interest in Egyptian themes makes an appearance in the works
of Piranesi and Comte de Caylus.

With such an onslaught the Rococo style gradually gave way
to these classical themes and surrendered to a second Renaissance of interest in antiquity. Architecture was the first to be
influenced. The first example of Neo-classicism in court circles
was the Pavilion de Louveciennes by Denise Ledoux which
was built for Madame du Barry in 1771. For the first time
chairs with horseshoe-shaped backs are displayed. Baron Grimm
writes in his *Correspondence Littèraire*, 1763, of the interior of
the house of the Classical Scholar Lalive de Jully which was
the first in Paris to be decorated in the Greek style with furniture
to match. Grimm states that for some years past antique forms
and ornament had been requested. "Tout est à Paris à la
Grecque."

It cannot be expected that all furniture assumed Classical
proportions and decorations immediately. As in all styles, there

One of a pair of Louis XVI beechwood chairs with an indistinct signature. Rectangular back with moulded frame-work, similar seat rails and fluted and reeded legs.

One of a set of six Louis XVI painted dining chairs, the moulded frame with lyre-shaped splats by anthemion motifs. Rounded stuffed seat, tapered and fluted legs.

was a period of transition of about ten years while the principles were being perfected. Ornament was the first to alter, followed by the line and structure, possibly based on the golden rectangle found in classical architecture. When the Louis XVI style was complete, its basis was the rectilinear line, and the curve of the circle and the arc replaced the Rococo curves. Cabriole legs were replaced by straight tapered legs.

The angular shape of the chair of the Louis XVI period is perhaps a little less comfortable than those of the previous reign, though the ornament is more varied. The most obvious difference between the two styles of chairs is that the Louis XV chair always has curved legs while the Louis XVI chair always has straight, tapered legs. As in all rectilinear chairs, the joints of the Louis XVI chair are always easily visible. Frames of these chairs are simply moulded or carved with running motifs such as beads, chains or Greek Key designs. The carving shows great refinement and delicacy. Chairs with oval or medallion backs often have a ribbon bow or a tiny floral wreath carved in the middle, accompanied by two sprays, bound with ribbon. A variety of shapes is used for the back of the fauteuil. Regardless of the general shape, if the back is slightly hollowed or shaped it is said to be *en cabriolet*. Perhaps the most characteristic of these backs are the *Medallion* and rectangular shape. The latter was designed in a number of ways. Some are square or almost square, others may have uprights that are either vertical or slope outwards. The cresting rail may be arched like a basket handle (*anse de panier*) or perhaps rectangular in form or slightly arched and sloped off at the angles

One of a pair of Empire mahogany armchairs. Bowed seat, square curved backs with horn-shaped arms resting on panelled uprights carved with bell flowers and the cabriole legs headed by winged ormolu griffins' heads. Ormolu paw feet, seat and backrail with ormolu laurel leaf mounts.

A rare Napoleon I mahogany fauteuil in the manner of Jacob Frères, with an over-scrolled leather-covered back and leather-covered squab seat, the arms in the form of winged griffins. Sabre back legs.

in a concave curve. These are called *en chapeau* (hat shaped), and often their uprights are slender columns detached from the main frame-work with perhaps carved finials in the shape of fir cones or feathers. Arms usually have manchettes, and are joined to the back in a curve that starts at the very top of the uprights of the back, usually terminating in a simple volute joined by the arm posts. Arm posts are always joined to the top of the straight legs and not often set back as in the previous period, but as panniers were still in vogue the arm posts curve inwards. Legs are moulded and taper towards the foot. Some are square in shape but others are round and turned with moulding at the top and a projecting moulding at the foot. Legs are often fluted vertically and sometimes spirally. A square is usually placed above the leg, joined for refinement to the seat rail and decorated on two sides with rosettes. Round legs are more popular for chairs than the square form, and are often given the name of quiver legs (*pieds en carquois*), though there may be no sign of feather terminals or a quiver. There was a fashion towards the end of the period, due perhaps to the interest in the antique, for the legs and arms to be joined in one piece. The comfortable bergères remained in great favour during the reign of Louis XVI. Their shape differs little from the fauteuil except for their closed arms, but some have gondola-shaped backs and have a continuous line from the end of one arm to the other.

Under the technical skill of such menuisiers as Louis Delanois, Jean Baptiste Sené, Nicholas Quimbert Foliot, Lelarge (see Chapter 4), Jean Baptiste Boulard, Jean Baptiste Tilliard and many others, chair design reached a very high standard. Wood carvers such as Georges Jacob (1739 to 1814) had perfected their skill. He was one of the greatest carvers of the eighteenth century and created some wonderful examples of craftsmanship in chairs, showing the evolution from the Louis XVI to the Empire style. Jacob is credited with introducing the lyre shape into furniture design and using it for chairs. He is also the first to use sabre legs, thus anticipating the Empire style, besides his use of mahogany (an example of the Anglomania sweeping France at the time) and closeness to Sheraton and Hepplewhite.

Chair backs were made out of wood, as open work was expensive to produce. They were made of mahogany, and painted and gilded—mahogany was introduced for chair making during this period. Many of these chairs were decorated with pierced splats (as in England) and were called *chaises à l'Anglaise*. The lyre shape was one of the most popular, but the sheaf back enjoyed quite a vogue with its bundle of rods spreading, fan-like, over the back. Some of the most novel chairs were those designed to celebrate the ballooning achievements of the brothers Montgolfier (whose first flight in a fire balloon had taken place in 1783) with a back shaped like a balloon. One can be seen at the Musée Carnavalet in Paris. The fashion for ladies to lie in a languorous manner on canapés and day beds continued as in the previous period and both the ladies and the day beds were still in great demand. Canapés were designed with solid or open sides as in the Louis XV period. These solid sides were often provided with seat cushions and appear more like a day bed or sofa, as their main use was for resting. The canapé retains the graceful lines of the Louis XV period but the curves are no longer sinuous and appear to be more under control. A new shape appears in a canapé called a *confident* which has at each end two shaped pieces that can be used as a seat. The point of the *canapé à confident* is that it enabled people to converse easily and it is a good example of furniture in the eighteenth century, being designed to meet the specific needs of social life.

The Directoire Style

The Directoire style owes its name to the Government of the Directors which lasted from 1795 to 1799. Like the Régence style it was not a complete style in itself. It retained much of the Louis XVI style and as it gradually evolved through the last few years of the eighteenth century it became the Empire style. A closer study of furniture from the ancient world had brought about the fashion for Greek furniture. Chairs with roll-over backs and other furniture closely copied from the antique were all becoming apparent before the Revolution of 1789. The Revolution did not bring about any rapid change in furniture

One of a pair of transitional chairs painted grey and signed "I. B. Sené" with a deeply moulded and cartouche-shaped back. Fluted tapering legs headed by paterae.

One of a pair of Empire mahogany arm chairs signed "Jacob Frères, rue Meslée". Back with a scrolled over-cresting, flattened arms resting on the heads of winged sphinxes.

Retour d'Egypte. One of a set of four fauteuils, the mahogany frames with square panelled backs and bowed seat covered in green leather. Outsplayed arms with curved and reeded supports, tapering front legs with carved gilt wood sphinx head terminals and paw feet.

design but it spurred on the style for antique designs which suited the tastes of the revolutionaries who admired ancient republics. However, in spite of the Revolution both the Directoire and the Empire styles produced a class of rich clients who appreciated luxurious interiors in the latest fashion just as much as the leaders of *ancien régime* society.

The transition from Louis XVI to Empire runs from about 1790 to 1804. Many pieces identified with the Directoire style still show the classical strictness of the Louis XVI style, often being more severe in line. Many pieces were copied straight from antique prototypes. The painter Jacques Louis David (1748 to 1825) declared: "We must go back to raw antiquity." Furniture decorated with antique ornament was not enough—it had to be exact copies from various excavations or from antique vase paintings. This was felt to be the correct style for the Republic and to adopt it was patriotic. David did much to establish this new taste. His ideas were far-reaching and politically influential. He engaged the skill of Jacob to make Greco–Roman models which he used in his paintings, and for designs. These were quickly copied by designers and painters. Many pieces were to become fashionable for domestic use. The curule-form chair with "X" supports, mahogany chairs with round backs and decorated with gilt bronze are copies of the Greek *Klismos* chair. The type of day bed with its graceful lines on which he painted Madame Récamier was also popular. The fashion for copying the ancient world brought about simplicity in clothes and hair styles for both men and women. David introduced two young architects and designers, who

Empire gilded stool.

were to have a lasting effect on the style and taste of the Empire period. Charles Percier (1764 to 1838) and Pierre Fontaine (1762 to 1853), under the leadership of Georges Jacob, were ordered to design the furniture for the Salle de la Convention at the Tuileries. After completing this work Jacob, a keen follower of antiquity, made his workshop over to his eldest sons in 1796, Georges and François Honoré, who took the name of Jacob Desmalter and became one of the great ébénistes of the Empire period (see Chapter 3).

The reign of terror brought about the suppression of Guilds which were dissolved in 1790. Instead of rules and regulations governing craftsmen there was complete freedom of production and, naturally, followed a decline in skill. As soon as the Revolution was over, workshops re-opened and most furniture grouped under the Directoire was made after 1795. The design was an imitation of the antique. The most famous interior of the time was that of Madame Récamier. Designed under the guidance of Percier and Fontaine in 7, Rue du Mont Blanc, mahogany was used for all the furniture, for the fittings, columns, architraves, doors and window frames. Mahogany became the fashionable wood and both chairs and day beds were made out of it with sweeping curves copying the Greek originals.

Symbolism was a great theme at this time. Many chairs and stools were made in the form of drums, and day beds in the shape of camp beds due to the military influence of the period. The fashion for Egyptian ornament owed much to the Egyptian campaign of Napoleon who took with him writers and archaeologists. Dominique Vivant de Denon (1747 to 1825) was one of

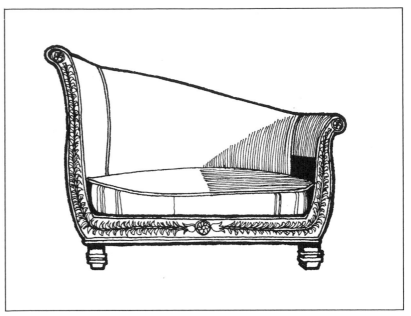

A small Empire mahogany bergère.   Empire Meridienne.

them, and gathered information for his book *Le Voyage dans la basse et la haute Egypte* published in 1802. It gave vivid descriptions of Egyptian ornament.

Directoire chairs were often painted in clear colours. The terminal part of the back began in a curling "S" form before becoming straight. Backs of chairs and armchairs were often upholstered and were sometimes ornamented with elegant motifs—in open work with a stylised version of the Louis XVI lyre shape. Armposts are baluster or columnar in form; front legs are turned round or tapering; arms end in small round knobs; volutes, if used, end in a square decorated with a carved daisy on the top. A typical motif is a small palm leaf or shell carved at the point where the arm joins the upright. Occasionally the armposts took the form of winged Sphinxes. Many chairs had open backs that rolled over and top rails were occasionally baluster shape. The most popular carved ornaments were stars, daisies, antique vases, fillet, and lozenges complete or with the corners cut off. Inspired by the Grecian couch the day bed was one of the most popular pieces to be connected with the Directoire period. It had equal roll-over ends and occasionally had a back.

The Empire Style

Napoleon established himself in 1790 as First Consul, though he did not become Emperor until 1804. He stated: "We must lay aside jackboots and think of commerce, encourage the arts, give prosperity to our country." He interested himself in forming a court and in finding palaces to house it, and these palaces were furnished in a manner suitable to his military achievements. He engaged the services of Percier and Fontaine who undertook all the conversions and redecorations of the palaces, houses and apartments lived in by Napoleon and Josephine, beginning with Malmaison on the outskirts of Paris, which Josephine had purchased in 1798. Both Percier and Fontaine established an immediate *rapport* with Napoleon and were able to interpret his feelings and ideas. They redecorated the Tuileries, Saint Cloud (which was later burnt down) and the Louvre in a style that depicted the epoch. It was during the time of the consulate that the Empire style made its début. Much of this emergence was due to the two geniuses, Percier and Fontaine, who were able to satisfy the aspirations to glory of Napoleon and to furnish his palaces to fit these ideas. Symbols of war formed a great part of the decorative themes. Napoleon found the Roman style of arts with its grandeur and solidity most suited to his ideas of power and prestige and favoured imperial emblems such as the eagle and figures of Victory as embellishments to his surroundings. Percier and Fontaine captured this feeling and created a style based on the antique which had both restraint and grandeur. The first Empire lasted from 1804 till 1814 but the style lasted ten or fifteen years after that date. Percier and Fontaine created a type of furniture with plain surfaces defined by straight lines and sharp edges, broken only by golden Greek palm leaves, wreathes and figures of Victory with outstretched wings, well suited to this Imperial period in French history. It was a style of austere grandeur conforming to the fixed ideas they had of the ancients and Imperial France. They wrote: "Simple lines, pure contours and correct shapes replace the miscelinear, the curving and the irregular."

Furniture would have been too severe if it had continued to be made in this manner, but the French ébénistes were quick to recognise the necessity for decoration. They added gilt bronze mounts to the dark shining surfaces of the mahogany and used practically all the motifs from Greco–Roman and Egyptian art. Although often borrowed from antiquity the animal kingdom was well represented. Sphinxes, chimeras, winged lions and eagles' heads were all used for decoration on table legs and armposts of chairs. Monopodia were used as table legs and swans served as armposts of chairs and sofas. There were many new lines in chair design. They are usually more severe than those of the Louis XVI period, being broad and simple, not always straight and many have roll-over backs resembling an "S" form. A type of seat that enjoyed great popularity during the Empire was the Gondola seat, characterised by a back arm-piece sloping backwards, and armrests that terminated in an abrupt manner giving the chair a graceful line when viewed sideways. A particularly attractive version is the gondola arm chair designed for Josephine by Percier and Fontaine which had

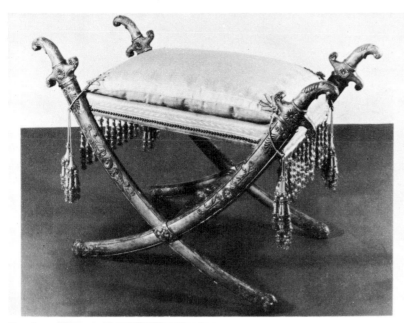

Empire military-type stool with sabre legs.

Empire desk chair in mahogany with gilt ornaments from the Victoria and Albert Museum.

two swans in the place left free by the concave line of the gondola.

The fauteuils of this period usually have upholstered seats and backs. Two types most frequently seen have rolled-over backs and are rectangular in form. Typical ornament for chairs is a palm leaf or shell decorating the point where the arm meets the upright, which is itself a direct continuation of the leg. These supports are often on elongated terminal figures. Front legs are usually straight, though they might sometimes be claw legs or decorated with spiral twists. Rear legs are often concave in form. The so-called sabre leg was not in use until after 1815. Chairs and stools were made in the ancient curule form with "X"-shaped supports. The bergères were a survival from the eighteenth-century arm chairs with a removable cushion and upholstery under the arms. Backs were altered to suit the new taste.

Sofas were no longer particularly distinguished, for they simply appeared as much larger versions of arm chairs or were entirely upholstered. There was a special type of sofa called *meridienne* which had two ends of equal height (as in David's portrait of Madame Récamier). These ends were joined by a straight backrest, but when the two end pieces were of unequal height the back piece would slope gracefully down from one end to the other. Sometimes, for convenience, the lower end of the meridienne could be folded down. The stool made a reappearance in court circles as Napoleon had decreed that arm chairs were to be reserved for the Empress Marie Louise of Austria, and his mother. All other members of the court had to sit on stools.

French Art Nouveau chair with mistletoe decoration.

Detail of cresting of a French Art Nouveau chair.

The Empire style affected most of Europe and was the last Classical era. It marks the end of the great age of French cabinet making. Modest furniture during this period is inferior to that of the eighteenth century—cabinet makers lowered their standards when the Guilds were dissolved, but finer pieces such as those made by Napoleon's favourite ébéniste, Desmalter, show remarkable skill and knowledge of materials. The introduction of the factory system, even in its simplified form, affected the standard of craftsmanship, and, as in the nineteenth century, industrialisation and mass-production brought about imitations of all periods and styles.

Queen Anne sofa with walnut frame, cabriole legs and pad feet, upholstered in yellow brocade. 1710

French Empire day bed in gilded mahogany, upholstered in blue silk.

70

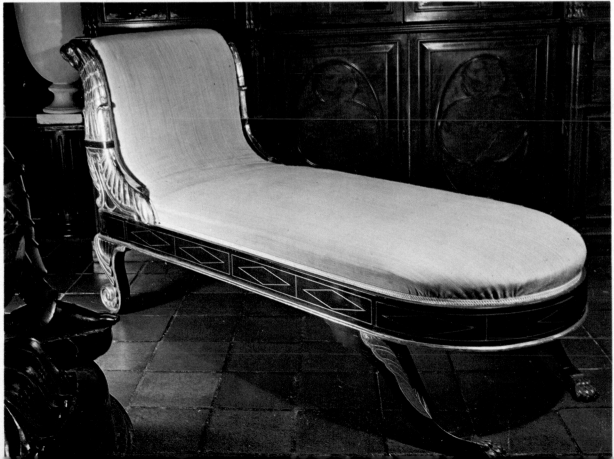

Chapter 3
The Age of the Ebéniste and Menuisier

The great age of the French ébéniste and menuisier was the eighteenth century. From the mid-seventeenth century ébénistes had been members of the Menuisiers Guild, but in 1743 this was renamed the *Corporation des Menuisiers-Ebénistes*. From this time cabinet making was divided into two groups. The menuisiers were responsible for making chairs, beds and other furniture constructed out of solid wood. The ébénistes adopted their name from the title *menuisier en ébéne* and were responsible for veneers and marquetry. In the eighteenth century there were more than one thousand maîtres who signed their work. In 1467 the first Guild statutes ordered the members of the corporation to sign their work but this order was not always kept and maîtres placed marks on their works. In 1741 the order was amended and all maîtres were compelled to possess an iron stamp with which he was to strike his name, or sometimes initials, on every piece of furniture which he put on sale. This even applied to pieces he might have had in to repair. As a rule a maître stamped his furniture on the underframing of chairs and tables or in any place where it could not spoil the appearance of the piece. When the Guilds were dissolved in 1790 the stamp was, of course, no longer necessary.

The stamp mark is the most important means of identifying the maker of French furniture during the last half of the eighteenth century. More detailed knowledge is possessed about French eighteenth-century craftsmen than their English counterparts due to the survival of many Guild records which have remained intact.

Pair of Louis XV chairs "en cabriolet". 1760–70

Menuisiers

A high degree of proficiency was maintained by the Guild and after many years of apprenticeship each prospective maître had to prove his ability by making a special piece of furniture which was judged by the Guild.

If successful, the applicant had to pay a large entrance fee. A maître could have several people to work with him and was by law obliged to have apprentices articled to him; he was also able to teach his sons and relations as well. Another interesting point is that a workman who married the widow of a maître, and even the widow herself if helped by suitable craftsmen, might run the workshop of her deceased husband.

To combat the competition from outside the Guilds, a law was passed in 1741 stating that each craftsman should mark his piece. Each mark was registered at a central office which added the stamp *J.M.E. Jurande* or *Juré des Menuisiers*. Not all signatures found today are clear; some are marks of the dealer who sold them or of the timber merchant. Nothing made before Louis XV was marked. Furniture for the crown was marked with the initials of the Palace and sometimes the room where it was to be placed.

Jean Avisse

Born 1723, became a maître in 1745, established at the Rue de Cléry. He was assisted by his wife Marie Anne Gourdin who came from a family of great menuisiers. His work was of outstanding quality and prices were so moderate that he attracted many furniture dealers and private customers. Despite this he went through a difficult financial period which he overcame and continued working until the Revolution when he was seventy-three years old.

He is best known for his fine Louis XV chairs, remarkable for their restrained design and elegance, though some are richly carved and a chair of his with tiny flowers can be seen in the Musée des Arts Decoratifs.

Pierre Bara

Became a maître in 1758, working with his cousin Charles Vincent Bara. They produced some outstanding chairs during the reign of Louis XV.

Blanchard

The name of one of the families of menuisiers in Paris. Nicholas Blanchard is the first to be mentioned and became a maître in

 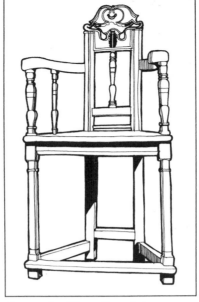

Louis XII chair with period moquette.   Caquetoire, Henry II period.

1738 and lived at Rue de Cléry. He was still in business in 1749. His signature is found on chairs made of walnut.

Jean Boucalt

Chair maker in Paris, born 1705, died 1786. He acquired his degree in 1728 and was established in the Rue de Cléry. Many of his chairs pass through the auction rooms.

Jean-Baptiste Boulard

Parisian menuisier, an official furniture maker to the Crown. He was born around 1725, died 1789, and gained his degree in 1754. He became established in the Rue de Cléry and acquired a reputation which made him eligible for the honour of being attached to the service of the *Garde Meuble*. He made pieces for Louis XVI. One of his principal achievements was a set of twelve pieces of very grand furniture for the study of the King at Versailles. He delivered chairs for the apartments of Madame Louise and Madame Elizabeth, sisters of Louis XV. The Comte d'Artois had him competé for the installation of the Chateau de Bagatelle and requested a set of eight large bergères. Boulard was often asked to mediate in professional trade disputes. His widow carried on his business after his death and continued to supply the royal household.

Boulard had two different signatures; one of these is found

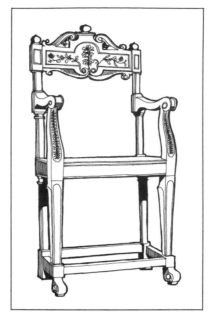
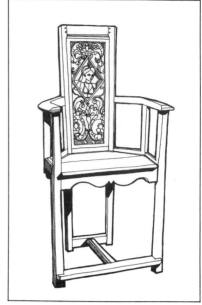

Henry II chair.

Caquetoire chair, late sixteenth century.

only on pieces of the reign of Louis XV. Many museums and private collections have examples of his work, including the Mobilier National, the Louvre and the Elysée Palace.

Sulpice Brizard

Born in 1735, died after 1798. He worked in Paris and gained his degree in 1763. He was married to Marie-Geneviève Meunier, daughter of an artisan in his field. Three years later he opened a workshop and produced chairs of exceptional quality. He is thought to have been one of the chief makers of seat furniture to the Crown during the reign of Louis XVI.

Louis Charles Carpentier

Obtained his degree in 1752 and worked during the reign of Louis XV. His chairs have a beautiful line and character. Examples can be seen in the Musée des Arts Decoratifs and the Musée Jacquemart-André in Paris.

Claude Chevigny

Became a maître in 1768 and was known for the luxurious chairs and other seat furniture that he made. He made a wonderful set of chairs for the Duc de Choiseuil at Chanteloup which is

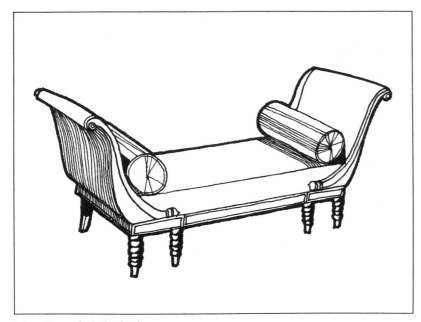

Mme Recamier's *lit de répos*.

now in the Chamber of Commerce buildings at Tours. The Mobilier National in Paris owns examples of his work, including some made for the Palais de Fontainebleau.

Louis Delanois

Born in 1731, died in 1792. He opened a small workshop in Rue Bourbon-Villeneuve in Paris. The fine work that he produced brought many furniture dealers of the time to the district and also many of the aristocracy such as the Prince de Beauvau and the Comte d'Orsay. He had the protection of Madame du Barry and furnished her lodgings at Fontainebleau. The chairs of her bedroom at Versailles were delicately carved with roses. Delanois had many noble patrons and grew to be very rich but the Revolution ruined him and he was declared bankrupt in 1790.

Jean Baptiste Bernard Demay

Acquired his degree in 1784 and worked in Paris for thirty years. At the beginning of his career he received orders for whole sets of furniture for the Queen, among which are some chairs with the monogram of Marie Antoinette, now in the Petit Trianon. At the Musée Carnavalet in Paris there are chairs catching the vogue of "ballooning à la Montgolfière", some of the backs being made in the shape of balloons. After the Revolution the signature of Demay was different as he included his address.

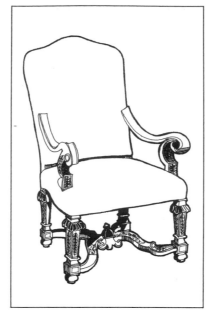

Louis XIV gilded arm chair.   Regency gilded wing chair.

Nicolas-Quimbert Foliot

Furnished the royal palaces with many pieces of furniture and made the base for Louis XV's Throne at Versailles and a whole set of furniture for the King's bedroom, which is now in the Musée du Louvre.

He was the son of Nicholas Foliot who had been official menuisier to the royal household from 1723 until his death in 1749 when Nicolas-Quimbert took over the workshop. His younger brother was a sculptor and was known as Foliot le Jeune. He left a son, Toussaint-François, who carried on the family business. Nicolas-Quimbert Foliot rarely marked his pieces but those that are marked usually bear the stamp of his father, F. Foliot.

Père Gourdin or Jean Gourdin

Was the first of that name to produce fine chairs and canapés. He worked between 1737 and 1763. His son, Jean-Baptiste Gourdin, became a maître in 1748 and had a business near to his father and worked for many of the nobles of the day. His chairs, like his father's, can be seen in many collections.

Michel Gourdin

Called Gourdin le Jeune; a brother of Jean-Baptiste, became a

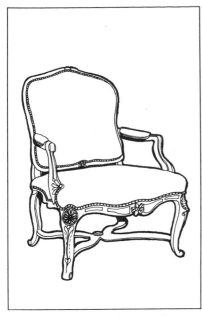

Regency arm chair with stretcher.

Traditional fauteuil with console leg by a Jacob.

maître in 1752 and made fine chairs in the Louis XV style.

Nicholas Heurtaut

Became a maître in 1755 and was established in Paris for over twenty years, producing beds and chairs of excellent quality.

The Jacob family

Were workers in hard wood for over a century. The first and greatest was Georges Jacob who was born in Cheny, Burgundy in 1739, and died in Paris in 1814.

He came to Paris at the age of sixteen to learn the art of wood-working and began with decorative sculpture, it is thought at the workshop of Louis Delanois. He became a maître in 1765, making as his chef-d'oeuvre a small model of an arm chair. From 1773 he received orders from the Garde Meuble Royal and was given the task of repainting some Boulle furniture. But he preferred to make chairs, beds, screens, consoles, etc. not only designing them but completing the carving himself. In this field he surpassed all his contemporaries. He had imagination and style, and created new forms. Chairs with round seats, console feet and lyre backs were among his innovations and he was the first to use mahogany for chairs. Marie Antoinette, for whom he executed many pieces, loved novelty and he created many pieces in the allegorical taste of the period.

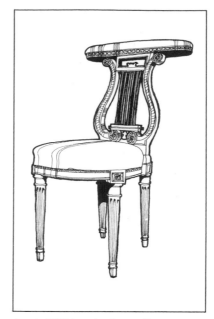
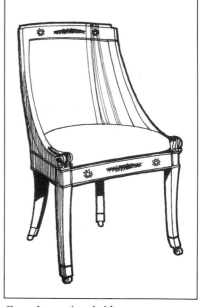

Louis XVI lyre-back voyelle
(cock fighting chair).

Consulate painted side
chair by Bernard.

Some very extravagant chairs were made for her boudoir at
Versailles. These chairs were designed with emblems such as
torches, quivers, sphinxes, symbols of mystery and fidelity as
well as the emblems of France and Austria—the cock and
eagle's heads. In the Musée des Arts Decoratifs in Paris there
are three chairs with the feet in the shape of quivers, arms in the
shape of horns, and backs decorated with the Austrian eagle
surmounted by roses. These chairs were designed for Marie
Antoinette's bedroom at Saint Cloud.

The painter Jacques Louis David copied his models from the
drawings on Etruscan vases. He wanted to have some furniture
of this type and nagged Jacob to make them. Made of dark
mahogany in order to simulate the patination of bronze, it was
from this that the Empire style was born. The friendship between
David and Jacob led to the launching of the new style. David's
political ideas helped and he arranged to have Jacob commis-
sioned to make the furniture for the new conference room in
the Palais des Tuileries. David designed the presidential seat.
The benches and stalls for the seven hundred and sixty
deputies were designed by the young architects Percier and
Fontaine, who had recently returned from studying in Rome,
but Jacob masterminded this mammoth task.

In 1796 Georges gave the direction of his business to his sons
Georges and François Honoré who were known under the new
order as Jacob Frères. Both were born in Paris—Georges in
1770 and François in 1768. The older was the administrator
and the younger the technician. He took the name of Jacob
Desmalter, the name of a small estate owned by his father in

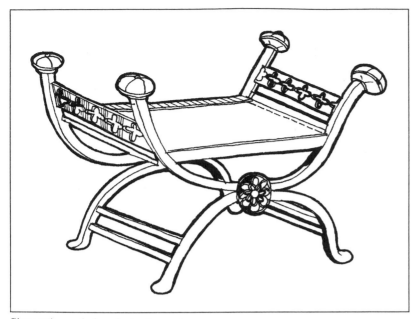

Siege episcopal-church stool.

Burgundy. He was a remarkable craftsman and was compared to Boulle and Riesener by his contemporaries. The brothers furnished many of the royal residences. They signed their work with a new stamp which included the street name. Many of these pieces still exist in France. They can be seen in the Musée des Arts Decoratifs and at Malmaison. Jacob Desmalter formed a business with his father. Jacob Desmalter & Cie had about fifteen workshops that produced a great deal of furniture for the royal estates and grand sets of chairs made to the designs of Percier and Fontaine. His son, Georges Alphonse Jacob Desmalter, born 1799, carried on the family tradition but in 1847 gave up making furniture due to the economic conditions and devoted his life to architectural drawing.

Jean-Jacques Pothier

Became a maître in 1750 and worked till 1780 making chairs and canapés which were of a beautiful shape and had graceful lines. His signature is found on a set belonging to the Mobilier National.

Jean Baptiste Tilliard (1685 to 1766)

A member of a family of furniture makers of unusual ability. He was a past master at making bergères and fauteuils, using crisp carving, often with a heart-shaped motif in the centre of

79

the back. The lines of his chairs are flowing and graceful yet retain a feeling of masculinity. Father and son worked for the royal household. The son, Jacques-Jean-Baptiste or Jean-Baptiste the Second, continued his father's tradition.

The signature of Tilliard was used by both father and son, so it may be concluded that pieces of an earlier date were made by the father and the later ones by the son who died in 1797. The best of their work was done between 1740 and 1760.

Chapter 4
American Chairs

In studying American furniture the chair has more relevance than any other item. This is because the chronological development of furniture styles is seen more clearly in chairs than in other articles and added to this is the fact that chairs were usually made in sets so there are many more to be seen than other pieces of furniture. It is often thought that American furniture is a wholesale imitation of English but this is only partly true. Early American furniture makers were indeed imitators, but only as far as structure and design were concerned. The finished article had usually been adapted to suit the developing American personality and its environment.

Remembering that a great many of the first settlers in America came from England, it is not surprising that they and their descendants should follow the English styles of furniture; what applies to English furniture applies also in some measure to its American counterpart, taking into account the adaptations made. It should also be borne in mind that style and taste took time to travel across the Atlantic and that America was sometimes more than a decade behind England in appreciating a new fashion in furniture and putting it to use. The first men and women to colonise America took very little with them in the way of supplies and belongings as storage space on the vessel would have been limited to food and other necessities. Accordingly, their first tasks were to erect shelters and construct some basic pieces of furniture essential for living. The settlers were far too concerned with elementary survival to spend hours on the skilled production of beautiful furniture so the first pieces, hurriedly thrown together, were crude and utilitarian. Very

Low-back side chair. Cromwellian-type chair. Upholstered. Oblong back and seat. Maple knob turnings. Plain oak stretchers at sides and back. Maine. 1650–1680

Side chair. Back has four sausage-turned vertical splats. Ball and sausage turnings on legs and stretchers. Rush seat. Red Mulberry. New Jersey. Late seventeenth century

Child's rocking chair. Painted pine rocking wing chair. Eighteenth century

few of these have survived.

But as the hardest times passed and colonies became established and began to prosper, people were less concerned with mere survival and could begin to appreciate the fruits of their labours. Cities such as New Amsterdam (later New York), Boston, Philadelphia, Newport and Baltimore began to spring up, and with them the furniture trade. Wealthy people were building large houses and were more than ready to pay for beautiful furniture with which to fill them. In the rural districts farmers, landowners and tradespeople were building smaller houses and were also buying furniture, possibly less pretentious but still tasteful.

In 1776 Independence was declared, and with it the birth of the "United States" of America. Ties of sovereignty with England were severed and America took her place among the nations of the world, but English influence continued to prevail in the American world of furniture.

Early Chairs—Colonial

The commonest form of early American chair had a seat of plain timber, rush or leather with turned legs and back supports.

Wainscot Chairs

These heavy oak chairs were among the earliest made by the

Side chair. Moulded stiles and crests, cowhide upholstery on back and seat. Block and vase turnings on front legs. Hour glass bulbous turnings on single front stretcher. Maple. 1700–1720

Corner chair. Spanish foot in front, the other feet turned. Transitional from William and Mary to Queen Anne period. Rush seat. Massachusetts. 1720

Side chair. Bannister back, rush seat, shaped carved crest rail and turned feet. Maple. Massachusetts. 1710–1720

settlers and were similar to ones in use in England at the time of James I. The wainscot illustrated has the panel and front stretcher made of oak while the other parts are made of maple. It has a scalloped crest rail which rises to two rounded crests in the centre, a high back, vase-turned legs and four plain stretchers. On several wainscots still in existence today the wooden seat has been replaced by leather. Although they were made in America by local craftsmen, many of these chairs were imported from England.

"Carver" and "Brewster" Chairs

These two chairs were named after their owners. The originals are to be found in the Pilgrim's Hall, Plymouth, Massachusetts and it is believed that they were actually taken to America on the *Mayflower*. John Carver, who died in 1621, was the first Governor of Plymouth which explains why the chair has a throne-like appearance. The original chair has turned uprights and plain, round stretchers joining the legs. The back has three horizontal turnings, the lower two being linked by three turned uprights. The seat is made of rush. This chair was copied until about 1700, later ones being rather lighter in weight and design.

William Brewster, 1567 to 1644, was an Elder of the Plantation. The Brewster chair is a little more elaborate than the Carver and copies are not as common. It is made from lengths of turning and has a rush seat. It has four rows of vertical turned spindles in the back, three rows on each side and two rows in the front.

Slat Back Chairs

The slat back chair shown here was made of ash in New England in the late seventeenth century. It has turned posts and spindles with four flat strips of wood running between the turned uprights at the back and greatly resembles a chair owned and used by William Penn and brought over from England. It was extremely popular in the colonies. There are many slat backs in existence which have rockers which had very often been added at a later date.

Banister Backs (William and Mary)

Banister back chairs came into general use in America in about 1700 to 1725. They were usually made of maple and were very popular for many years particularly in country districts. The spindles in the back were usually one half of a round banister called a "split banister". These were made by taking two pieces of wood and gluing them together temporarily with a strip of paper between to prevent them from adhering too firmly. The turning was then done on a lathe before the two pieces were separated ready to be fitted into the chair. The flat part faced the seat for the greater comfort of the sitter. Another feature of the banister backs was the carved crestings and legs and bulbous stretchers.

Corner Chairs

This corner chair was made from 1720 onwards and was popular at the same time as banister back chairs. This particular chair is a good example of the transitional period between the William and Mary and Queen Anne style. It has a rush seat, turned uprights and bulbous turned legs and stretchers. The front foot is Spanish and the others are turned.

Queen Anne Chairs (1730 to 1760)

Queen Anne's reign was short, lasting from 1702 to 1714, yet the style in furniture to which she gave her name was fashionable for many years after her death. The style became popular in America around 1730, slightly after England, and continued to be so until about 1760. The noticeable changes that came with the advent of the Queen Anne style was that the formal lines of former chairs were abandoned for a more graceful and elegant approach. We see the beginnings of the cabriole leg, the claw and club and ball foot and of course the increase in the use of mahogany.

The two Queen Anne chairs illustrated here are early examples,

Elbow chair. Old black paint and rush seat. Bannister back. Maple. Massachusetts. 1720–1730

Child's high chair. Wood not specified. Connecticut. 1730–1740

Child's high chair. Rush seat, ladder back with turned posts and stretchers. Bannister back. Finials at the arm and post ends are lemon shaped. Maple. Connecticut. 1730–1740

made in 1740, of walnut. The backs of both curve at the ends of the top and have a concave curve in the centre. The splats, which are "fiddle" or "rose" shaped, rest upon the rear seat rails. (Later Queen Anne chairs and, of course, Chippendale's, featured pierced splats.) Both these chairs have cabriole legs and Dutch club or pad feet. The most prominent feature is the cyma curve (consisting of a concave and convex line) which is present in almost every part of the chair. Both these examples were made in Massachusetts.

There is an interesting difference between Queen Anne chairs made in New England and those made in Philadelphia. Cabinet makers in Philadelphia followed the English practice of joining the side and front seat rails together in a deep joint and then pegged the front leg into it. This meant the seat rails were narrower at the front because they no longer were tenoned into the corner posts. The seat could now curve out over the front legs so that it was possible to peg the leg in from below. In New England this idea was, on the whole, not adopted and seat rails continued to be tenoned into the tops of the front legs.

New England Queen Anne chairs were usually made of walnut. This was also the case at first in Philadelphia until about 1745 when mahogany became almost exclusively used. The most unusual easy chair with its straight rounded legs and pad feet is an example of country craftsman's work in New England in about 1740 to 1750 when the taste for Queen Anne style was in vogue.

Side chair (one of a pair). Shaped
crest rails, solid splats, turned
stretchers, cabriole legs, pad feet,
balloon-shaped seat. Indigo-resist
covering. Walnut.
Massachusetts. 1730–1740

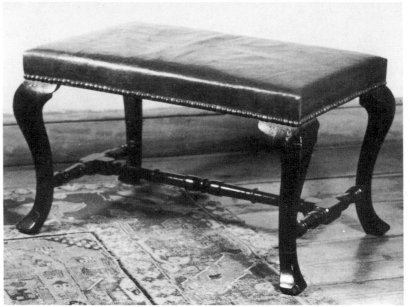

Stool. Upholstered. Turned stretchers and square Dutch-type Queen Anne
feet. Walnut.
Rhode Island. 1730–1750

Chippendale Style Chairs (1755 to 1785)

The Chippendale style of chair, so popular in England, was
probably first adopted in America in 1755 and was most closely
followed and highly developed in Philadelphia. From 1755 to
1785 most of the best furniture was made in this style and continued to be very popular in America when Adam and Hepplewhite styles prevailed in England. This was due mainly to the
fact that the Revolutionary war and the Declaration of
Independence made contact less viable between the two countries in the fields of art and fashion.

At about this time there emerged a group of furniture makers
known in some circles as the American Chippendales. William
Saveny of Philadelphia is noted for the chairs and other furniture
he made "at the sign of the chair, a little below the market in
Second Street, Philadelphia" (these words were found on a
lowboy made by Saveny). He was a Quaker who sold much of
his work to other wealthy Quakers in Philadelphia. His clients
were ready to pay well for their purchases so Saveny spared
few pains in making liberal use of the cabriole leg, the claw and
ball foot, the fiddle back and the ornamentally turned stretcher.
Elaborate carving features little in his work. Benjamin Randolph
was another American furniture maker who concentrated
entirely on chairs. Collectors and specialists believe that the
chairs he produced are amongst the finest ever made in America.
He sold his chairs to the wealthiest Philadelphians who highly
appreciated the carved cabriole legs and the ribbon tracery of
the backs. Perhaps his greatest work was the manufacture

Louis XV fauteuil upholstered in
sixteenth century spanish material.
1735

Easy chair. A unique easy chair, straight rounded legs and pad feet. An example of the country craftsman's work. New England. 1740–1750

Side chair. Shaped crest rail, solid splats, turned stretchers, cabriole legs and pad feet. Scalloped ogee skirt. Upholstered wool flamestitch. Walnut. Massachusetts. 1740–1750

Side chair. Slip-in seat, serpentine crest rail with reeded ears. Interlaced splat. The two lower "curlicues" have been restored. The reeded square moulded legs are stop fluted. Four plain square moulded stretchers. Mahogany. Newport, Rhode Island. 1760–1770

of "six simple chairs" discovered at the beginning of this century.

Shown here are two typical examples of American Chippendale side chairs made between 1766 and 1770. The first features a shaped, carved crest rail with the back splat carved with tassel, ruffle and acanthus leaf. The front seat has gadroon moulding and the cabriole front legs have acanthus leaf carving and terminate in ball and claw feet. It has a slip cushion or drop-in seat and is made from mahogany. The other is also of mahogany and has a shaped and yolk scrolled crest rail with shaped stiles. The open work interlaced splat is ornamented with volutes and scrolls. It features a balloon-shaped slip seat and frame on cabriole legs which are braced with baluster turned lateral and bilateral stretchers above ball and claw feet.

A third mahogany side chair is also shown. It has a serpentine crest rail with reeded ears and an interlaced splat. On the reeded square moulded legs the fluting stops just above the four plain square moulded stretchers.

Wing Chairs

Wing chairs were popular in pre-revolutionary days and were made and used all over the country. They were not indigenous to any particular area. Shown here is an elegant wing chair made in New England in about 1770. It has a mahogany frame with pine, tulip wood and oak used as secondary woods, and has a shaped, rounded crest rail with shaped wings and rolled arms. The square front legs are stop fluted and the chair is

Wing chair. Inlay on straight tapering mahogany legs, pronounced serpentine top (the centre stretcher has been replaced). New Hampshire, 1790

87

Day bed. Maple, red-painted with turned stretchers and square-type Dutch feet. The solid splat back and curved crest rail suggest Queen Anne, while the posts and spindles suggest a hold-over from the William and Mary period. Some restoration.
Rhode Island? 1740–1750

Day bed with indigo-resist covering. Walnut. Massachusetts. 1750–1760

upholstered with brass studs. A slightly later chair made in 1790 is also featured. It has straight tapering legs and a pronounced serpentine top. The centre stretcher is not original.

In England, Chippendale style was succeeded by the designs of Robert Adam and Hepplewhite. For many reasons the Adam style of furniture was never made in America, the most important being that it became popular in England during the American Revolutionary war when business relations were suspended, so American cabinet makers continued in the Chippendale style. When business between the two countries was resumed after 1783, Hepplewhite was taking the place of Adam in England and America moved from Chippendale to Hepplewhite thus taking little notice of Adam.

Hepplewhite (1780 to 1792)

Hepplewhite furniture was imported into America from about 1780 and soon became popular enough for cabinet makers to imitate the style. It was especially developed in Baltimore where it was extremely popular. A chair of particular importance is the Baltimore Shield Back Chair made from mahogany in 1790. The inlaid eagle medallion is a symbol of the then newly acquired American Independence. There is a shell segment at the base of the splat and as a whole the shield-shaped back is well designed and executed.

Easy chair. Mahogany frame (pince, tulipwood and oak secondary woods). Shaped, rounded crest rail with shaped wings and rolled arms. Square stop fluted front legs. Upholstered with brass studs.
Rhode Island. 1770

Elbow chair. Martha Washington type. Mahogany, upholstered back and seat. Back has serpentine top. Arms moulded, tapering front legs fluted. Four plain stretchers.
Late eighteenth century

Sheraton Style, 1795 onwards

In 1791 Sheraton published in England the first section of his book *Cabinet Maker's and Upholsterer's Drawing Book* and his style of chairs came into vogue there in 1792 to 1795. It is probable that the style came into fashion in America during the next two or three years, but American Sheraton chairs do not always closely follow the designs in Sheraton's book. Any chair therefore, having any of the main Sheraton features, especially the square back, is classified as being a Sheraton chair.

Two examples of square back Sheraton chairs are illustrated here. The first was made in Massachusets in the late eighteenth century of mahogany with traces of gilding. The back is nearly square except for the arched top rail and the uprights are reeded. There are three vertical splats, each of which is divided in the centre to enclose an oval rosette. The tapered front legs are fluted and the four stretchers are plain. The seat is upholstered. The second chair was made of mahogany in about 1802 by Slover and Taylor in New York. The centre of the top splat features a rectangle with a carved daisy as normally used by this firm. It has an upholstered seat, reeded legs and spade feet.

Duncan Phyfe (or Neo-Greek Style)

Perhaps one of the greatest names in American furniture design is that of Duncan Phyfe. He was born in Scotland in 1768 and went to New York in 1783 with his parents. He learned his

89

Rocking chair. Five-slat elbow chair. Original red-orange painted graining and original rockers. Pennsylvania. 1765–1760

Side chair. Mahogany ladder-back chair with slip-in upholstered seat. Horizontal splats with circular ornament in centre. Attributed to Daniel Trotter. Philadelphia. 1785

Elbow chair. Martha Washington type. Upholstered seat and back. Reeded arms, tapering square legs. Possibly cherrywood. Rhode Island. 1790–1800

trade outside New York but returned there in 1789 as a joiner, and started his own business in Broad Street in 1795. He rose rapidly to fame, and by the age of thirty was well established and regarded as one of the foremost designers and makers of fine furniture by the fashionable people of the day. His best work was probably done around the turn of the century when New York was becoming a city of notable commercial enterprise which brought increasing wealth to many of its inhabitants. More and more fine houses were being built and Duncan Phyfe was given plenty of trade. He had the ability of sensing exactly what his clients wanted and accordingly produced the elegant and distinctive furniture which has made him famous.

In the years of his best work he followed Sheraton, Hepplewhite and Chippendale, adding his own variations to their basic designs. All these he combined to make a style which was instantly recognisable. It is said that Duncan Phyfe chairs were of few types but the variations were chiefly in the decorations which consisted mainly of carving, veneering and reeding. Having covered all phases of the Neo-classical style from Sheraton and Hepplewhite to Directoire, Empire and Victorian, he retired in 1847. He made most of his chairs of mahogany, employing the use of the lyre back, the grecian urn, the crossbar back and rosettes for decoration. The acanthus leaf in all shapes and sizes was used liberally on front legs and on the bowl sections of supporting pedestal urns. He often put brass shoes on feet (a practice well known in France but rarely used in England) and he also used casters on sofas.

During his most successful years he employed over one

Sheraton type side chair. Mahogany with traces of gilding, upholstered seat. Three vertical splats each divided in centre to enclose an oval rosette. Massachusetts. Late eighteenth century

Baltimore chair, one of a pair, features an inlaid eagle medallion on the characteristic central splat and shell segment at the base. Mahogany. 1790–1800

Baltimore chair. This chair, one of a pair, features an inlaid eagle medallion on the central splat and shell segment at the base. This type of back very characteristic of the Baltimore style. Mahogany. 1790–1800

hundred workmen and also had his own lumber yard. He imported the finest Santo Domingo and Cuban mahogany for which he paid enormous prices. The veneer he used was cut under his supervision and was applied with "Peter Cooper's Best Glue".

An example of a Sheraton-style Duncan Phyfe chair is shown here. This chair, one of a set of six, features the cross bars in the back with the carved rosette in the centre. It has a rounded and reeded seat rail and reeded and tapering legs. The top rail is carved with one of Phyfe's favourite designs known as the "thunderbolt" (which resembles a fireburst).

Another example given is a mahogany Empire style sofa attributed to Duncan Phyfe. The seat, three-panel back and curved arms are caned. The crest rails of the back and arms are curved and carved laurel branches can be seen in the centre back and arm panels. The reeded legs form a crossed reverse curve and the feet terminate in casters hidden in brass paws. There are brass masks at the intersections of the arches of the legs and brass finials at the end of the rails.

American Empire Style (1805 to 1840)

The American Empire Style was developed from the English and French Empire styles. The best Empire style furniture was made in New York between 1815 and 1830, after which its elegance and character sadly declined. The better Empire furniture was then replaced by rather heavy bulky styles which,

Side chair. Mahogany chair with Sheraton back. In centre of top splat is a rectangle with carved daisy as used by Slover and Taylor. Vertical splats form Gothic arches and have "leaf" capitals. Reeded legs, spade feet, upholstered seat. Attributed to Slover and Taylor.
New York City. 1802–1804

Sofa. Mahogany frame. Crest has central panel carved with tassels and swags, flanked by rows of vertical fluting. Reeded arms curve down on to columnar reeded supports. Four tapering reeded legs, brass casters (old bust replacements). Upholstered in striped gray, blue and gold sprigged satin. Length four feet. New York. 1815

like the Victorian styles, had no really outstanding features. Thus "American Early Empire" style chairs are known as the best of the period whereas "American Later Empire" style refers to the poorer work executed after 1830. As far as the Empire chairs are concerned, few bear much resemblance to the style of the French Empire of Napoleon.

Fancy Chairs

It was during the early American Empire period that the Fancy Chair became fashionable. It was English in origin and was thought to have been introduced by Sheraton in an attempt to adapt the French mode of the early days of Napoleon to English taste. The English showed little interest in this new venture but the American chair makers seized on it and made it a trade all by itself. Fancy Chairs were soon found in shops all over America and were even "exported" to the French colonies in the South. They were later made for export, chiefly to the West Indies. In design the Fancy Chair was simple, but it was the decoration which made it so successful. The frame was usually painted black, relieved with reddish lines to imitate graining and then gilt striping and stencilling were used. The designs were usually the rather conventional leaves and fruit but also included houses, fountains and birds.

Lambert Hitchcock of Connecticut is the most noted maker of Fancy Chairs. He began his career by making chair parts for shipment to South Carolina but by 1821 his water-power-

Hitchcock "fancy chair" with painted and stencilled decoration. Found in the Hudson Valley, New York.
First half of nineteenth century

Side chair (from a set of six). Because of climate, the finish is varnish, not wax polish. Attributed to Duncan Phyfe. Greek revival, American empire dining-room. 1800–1820

Decorated side chair. Balloon seat and balloon back. Reddish brown with an intricate floral pattern on the crest, the splat and the leading edge of the seat. Extensively banded with yellow paint.
Pennsylvania. 1820

driven shop known as Hitchcockville had begun to produce Fancy Chairs. At first the chairs were labelled "L. Hitchcock, Hitchcockville, Connecticut" but in 1829 after bankruptcy Hitchcock took Alfred Alford as a partner to boost his finances and the label changed to "Hitchcock, Alford and Co." This label is stencilled on the back seat rail of the example shown here. A further example features a Fancy Chair made in 1820 in Pennsylvania which has a balloon seat and back, and is painted with a base of reddish brown. It has an intricate floral pattern on the crest of the splat and front seat edge. It is banded all over in yellow paint.

Windsor Chairs (see also Chapter 5)

Windsor Chairs were, of course, English in origin and were introduced in America, where they were highly developed, in about 1725. At first they were known as Philadelphia chairs but this soon gave way to the name by which they are known today.

The plainer types were obviously cheaper and were usually found in farmhouses or more modest dwellings. The better type of Windsor was bought by wealthy people but not usually placed in drawing-rooms. The first sort of Windsor had a low back but variations were soon added, including the comb back, hump back, bow back, fan back and the writing chair. All these were made with or without arms.

The Comb Back Chair is low backed with an extension of spindles supporting a built-on comb. The one illustrated features

One-slat dining chair. After meals or when the floor was being cleaned the chairs were pushed under the table or hung on the peg board. The Hancock chairs were first used after the pine forms were discarded. 1810–1820

Three-slat side chair. Made for use at a high counter or ironing table. The acorn finials are typical of mid-century New Lebanon craftsmanship. 1840–1850

Painted side chair. Hitchcock, Alford & Co. Stencilled on the back seat rail is "H. A. & Co. Hitchcocks-ville, Conn. Warranted." 1830–1840

a crest rail with spiral ears and a seven spindle comb back. The arms, legs and stretchers are vase-turned. Another illustration shows a painted fan-back elbow chair with knuckle arms. The two uprights in the centre back, the two end arm supports and legs have vase and ring turnings. It is thought that Fan Backs were made as side chairs to Comb Backs as the top rails of both chairs are similar. Both these chairs were made in the late eighteenth century.

The Bow Back made in the nineteenth century and painted Hump Back made in 1785 were also made as side chairs to go with arm chairs.

An unusual Windsor writing chair made between 1780 and 1790 is shown here, the remarkable feature being the low back; most Windsor writing chairs had high backs and comb tops. This particular chair is of green painted wood with plain slat back, turned legs and stretchers. The oval-shaped writing surface has a drawer underneath the seat. On others the writing arm is on a pivot so that it can be swung towards the writer. Some left-handed Windsor writing chairs are to be found, but they would originally have been specially ordered and made and are most unusual.

The most noticeable difference between English and American Windsor chairs is that the English backs very often had a pierced splat in the centre back whereas the American backs had only spindles. The legs of the English Chair are usually placed at the corners of the seat while American legs are more slanting.

Painted side chair. Hitchcock, Alford & Co. Stencilled on the back seat rail is "H. A. & Co. Hitchcocks-ville, Conn. Warranted."
1830–1840

Sofa. The feet terminate in casters hidden in brass paws, and there are brass masks at the intersections of the arches of the legs, and brass rosette finials at the ends of the rails. Mahogany, Empire style. Attributed to Duncan Phyfe. New York City. 1815–1825

Rocking Chairs

Historians believe that the Rocking Chair was an American invention, as the same chair did not emerge in Europe until long after it was well established in America. The earliest form of rocking chair usually had a slat back. The red and orange rocking chair illustrated was made in Pennsylvania in 1765 and has the original rockers.

The first rocking chairs were often other types of chairs adapted by shortening the legs and adding the rockers. They then became so popular that rocking chairs in the style of Windsor chairs and Fancy Chairs became a trade in their own right during the nineteenth century. All forms of Windsor, slat back, banister back, lyre back and Fancy Chairs are to be found with rockers, mostly original but some have rockers added at a later date.

A later rocking chair, made in the first half of the nineteenth century, is also shown. It is painted yellow and has a cane seat. On the top splat is a beautiful hand painted bowl of fruit surrounded by leaves and moss roses. The lower splat is a decorated combination of hand painting and stencil.

Shaker Furniture

It would not be right to leave American chairs without some reference to the Shakers and their contribution to American furniture.

The Shakers were a religious community formed in New Lebanon, New York, as the United Society of Believers in Christ's Second Coming. Led by Mother Anne Lee, a self-appointed priestess, these men and women withdrew from the world to live in communities run on the lines of pure theoretical communism. At its peak, between 1840 and 1860 there were eighteen such communities with a total of as many as six thousand members. The Shakers believed in a strictly non-indulgent life; they were pacifists and also took a vow of celibacy which may account for the eventual disappearance of the sect. Despite this they have left behind them their mark in the history of American furniture. They believed in a simple, utilitarian yet perfect style and each piece of work was executed with workmanship of the highest possible standard.

Everything about the Shakers was uncluttered. Chairs were the straight slat-back type as is the Shaker Rocking Chair made from cherrywood in 1820. This sturdier chair was made for the Brethren as opposed to the Sisterhood (who sat on even simpler one slat chairs). The rocking chair has the usual four slats and is a beautiful piece of craftsmanship. The Shakers, who received their name from a fast ritual dance performed every Sunday evening, kept the surfaces of their furniture as smooth as possible, never obscuring it with heavy veneers or varnishes and using only wax to make the grain of the wood show through. The lines were straight and the effect of the patina beautiful.

Victorian Furniture

Victorian furniture brought no fresh inspiration and no formal patterns but resurrected ideas from the past. A good deal of Victorian furniture was made by John Henry Belter in his New York workshop between 1840 and 1860. Rather ornate in style with Rococo themes, he made chairs and settees with pro-nounced curves and open work carving, obtaining strength by the use of an interesting lamination process. Thin layers of wood built up, with the grain of the wood in every other piece running in the opposite direction. It was then glued together and cut out. Examples of his work are a side chair and love seat made out of rosewood in 1855. These can be seen at the American Museum at Bath in England.

Chapter 5
Windsor Chairs

The Windsor Chair

The Windsor chair is a traditional chair popular in both America and England. It first appeared at the end of the seventeenth century and gave scope to many national features, though basically it was made in two forms, the *Hoop Back* and the *Stick Back* or *Comb Back*. In the Hoop Back the turned spindles were set into sockets in a hoop-shaped frame, and also into a solid wood seat. The turned legs were set into sockets under the seat and strengthened by simple stretchers. The Stick Back or Comb Back had a back curved like a comb or yoke into which the spindles were socketed. The method of construction led to both chairs being widely called Stick Back chairs. The seats were usually of elm and the bentwood parts of ash, yew or beech. Legs were usually turned, but by the mid-eighteenth century the design of the cabriole leg was familiar to country craftsmen and was used occasionally on the front legs which ended in a pad or hoof foot. However, stretchers were not discarded as they were with the more fashionable cabriole-legged chairs. The stretchers usually run from the front leg to the back and across the middle, to form a horizontal "H" beneath the seat. The crinoline or cow horn stretcher bends inwards from the front leg to meet two short bars attached to the back legs which hold the stretcher.

The term Windsor has for many years been derived from a hazy legend that George III had favoured such a chair made in the locality of Windsor, but research has shown that Windsor chairs were known in the early years of the eighteenth century

Windsor chair with writing arm. Green-painted wood. Plain slat back, turned legs and stretchers. Oval-shaped writing surface with drawer underneath. 1780–1790

Windsor comb back arm chair. Crest rail has spiral ears. Seven-spindle comb back. Knuckle arms. Vase-turned arms, legs and three splats. Windsor fan-back elbow chair. Painted fan-back elbow chair with knuckle arms. Late eighteenth century

well before the King was born. The place usually associated with their manufacture is High Wycombe, Buckinghamshire, where they are still made in large numbers. The Windsor chair was widely popular in the eighteenth and nineteenth centuries and many were exported to America after which the chair was also made locally there in various forms of comb back, and under a variety of labels ranging from *Philadelphia Windsor* to the *New England Comb Back*. In England the chairs were not confined to cottages and farm houses, but were often used in tea and coffee houses and were painted green, yellow and red. They were also to be found in lavishly furnished houses.

The search for novelty in shape and decoration led to many variations in the design of the backs of these chairs. A central splat was introduced which strengthened the structure and also enabled decorative piercings to be made. Some chairs had a back with a circular or wheel shape, or circular shape with the sticks or spokes radiating from a solid or pierced hub.

The Windsor chair was also made as a rocking chair, in which form it acquired considerable popularity. Thomas Jefferson, the American President, is said to have written the first draft of the Declaration of Independence in 1776 seated in a version of the Windsor chair which he designed himself.

The effect of contemporary fashions can be seen in the details of the design of the Gothic variety. The spindles were replaced by splats carved with a design in Gothic tracery, enclosed as in a pointed arch which replaced the turned supports. The size of the chair ranges from the large "grandfather" model to the armless kitchen chair that is frequently seen. It is unlikely that

English Windsor chair with decorated splat and crinoline stretcher. Yew and beechwood.

Late-eighteenth-century painted ladderbacks. Peter Bernard.

one will find matching sets; sometimes one sees two or three alike, but rarely more. Some of these plainer, cheaper chairs can look very attractive painted or lacquered in bright colours. Windsor chairs are still reasonably cheap although the ones made of yew are more expensive and are the most sought after.

A variation of the Windsor chair is the *Mendlesham chair*, so called because it was made by a Suffolk chair maker, Dan Day, who worked at Mendlesham and Stoneham in the late eighteenth century.

Country Chairs

A *Ladder Back* chair, which was usually found in Lancashire, appeared late in the seventeenth century and was called the Dutch chair. However, they can in fact be traced back to the fourteenth century. The back slats run horizontally between the uprights like rungs on a ladder. They are usually plain and rough, though on superior models they may be shaped into a wavy line and are occasionally pierced. Early examples have low backs, but later ones have a thin narrow back. In the country districts the woods used were mostly ash, elm, walnut, beech and oak. The seats were either plain or rush. Legs are sturdy looking and turned and the back legs continue upwards to form the back. They were adopted by town chair-makers, who gave them refinements such as dipped seats and slats shaped like a cupid's bow.

Amongst the simplest form of eighteenth-century chair is

Mid-eighteenth-century elm ladderback arm chair. Dark and Rendlesham.

Simple country spindle-back chair. Elm.

that which is known as the *Spindle Back*. These were made in large numbers all over England on the same lines as the Ladder Back. They have two rows of five vertical spindles and, though they vary in shape and thickness are generally turned; seats are more often than not made of rush and the foot is a rough survival of the ball and claw foot.

Chapter 6
Art Nouveau

Art Nouveau was both a style and a movement ahead of its time. It evolved at about the same time as the Arts and Crafts movement. Whether it was called *Secession* in Austria, *Stile Liberty* in Italy, *Le Style Moderne* or *Yachting Style* in France, *Jugenstil* in Germany, or just plain Art Nouveau in England and America, it was all part of one aesthetic movement that set out to change the style of architecture and the decorative arts. It was William Morris's taste for simple, straightforward and lifelike designs that inspired many Art Nouveau artists at the beginning and these were to be the main themes after the more bizarre ideas had been exhausted. Art Nouveau was not an isolated phenomenon as it had already been apparent in the Gothic revival and the Arts and Crafts Movement, and it continued into the Bauhaus Movement. The main theme of Art Nouveau was nature, already a character of mid-Victorian taste of which John Ruskin was a leading protagonist. It was in Art Nouveau that nature became an overpowering decorative and constructional theme. In order to free themselves from the past, Art Nouveau artists abandoned the accepted principles of design and construction. They were often unaware of the nature of materials—wood and metal were formed into tortured naturalistic shapes structurally as well as decoratively.

Much Art Nouveau furniture has an aspect of novelty which makes it appear unrelated to the history of design in furniture. The style was most fashionable between 1895 to 1905, and reached its height in 1900 when there were two exhibitions in Paris and Vienna. It is a link between historicism and the modern movement and the foundation of the Bauhaus in 1919. The

Oak rush-seated chair designed by C. F. A. Voysey and made by Story & Co. Victoria and Albert Museum. 1899

Painted dining-room chair. 1925

In the late nineteenth century an idea was revived for garden furniture, basket work. This had a great vogue during Edwardian times and early part of the twentieth century.

Martha Washington chair, with high rounded balloon shaped back, shaped arms with inlaid banding and reeding, and slightly bulbous forelegs. Upholstered in contemporary cotton chintz. Massachusetts, late eighteenth century

style shows the influence of Rococo, Gothic, Baroque and Japanese Art. Both Liberty (founder of the famous shop in London) and Samuel Bing state that they were influenced by the Orient. Samuel Bing's shop in Rue Provence, Paris, opened in December 1895; it was called Maison de l'Art Nouveau, giving a name to the movement which was generally accepted by 1900. Bing's shop was the clearing place for the latest pieces in the style, and was the centre for such artists as Eugène Galliard, Eugène Collona, Georges de Feuré, Charpentier, Plumet and many others. The main theme adopted by these artists was that of the *Style Metro*. The architect Hector Guimard was perhaps the most imaginative worker with this style exemplified in the iron grill work of the metro stations in Paris.

Another important contribution to French Art Nouveau was the School of Nancy. The central figure there was Emile Gallé, who lived from 1846 to 1904, whose vases, glass and furniture were considered first-rate works of art. Looking at them it can be seen that he had the typical sympathy of many Art Nouveau artists—sympathy for nature. He was France's greatest naturalist. At Nancy there was a close affiliation with the Rococo style and Art Nouveau, as many Art Nouveau artists were stimulated by the Rococo buildings of the eighteenth century to be found there. Also working at Nancy were Louis Majorelle and Eugène Vallin. Gallé's furniture was often in very natural forms—its structure took the shape of branches and stalks. Louis Majorelle's furniture is less complicated and more plastic and the shapes are full of movement.

After the *Exposition Universal* in Paris in 1900, Art Nouveau

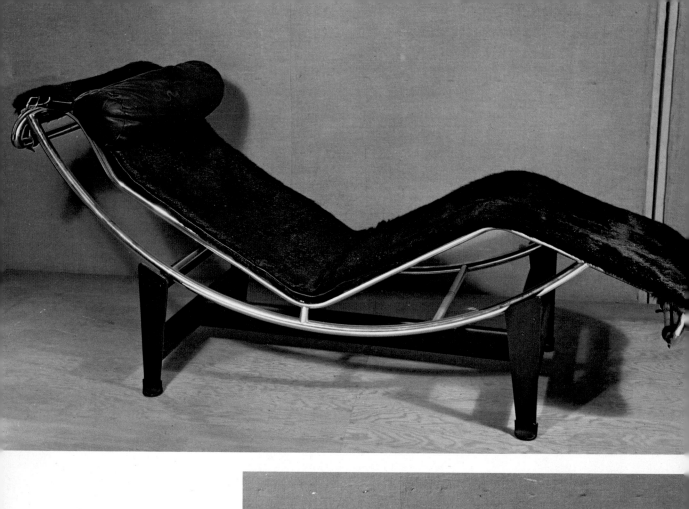

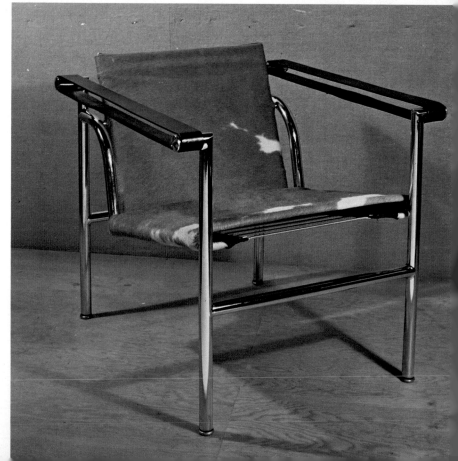

These basket chairs were in great demand for conservatories and gardens. Some pieces are made in this material today.

Polished cast iron garden seat. 1850–1860

appeared to become very complex and excessive in line. Artists were gradually to adopt a more restrained format for furniture, more in keeping with French period furniture. By 1910 a simplified modern classicism inspired by Directoire and Empire styles was adopted, foreshadowing the fashion in the 1920s. Chairs followed the natural line of other furniture and are easily recognised by the contorted branch-like shapes favoured in France at this time. Many woods were used—mahogany and walnut both stained green, and carved and gilded wood.

One of the main centres in Britain for Art Nouveau was Glasgow, where the movement was led by a Scottish architect Charles Rennie Mackintosh (1868 to 1928). Mackintosh, Herbert Macnair and the Macdonald sisters Frances and Margaret formed the Glasgow Four in 1891, a group of people who all seemed to evolve their ideas at the same time when many sources were available to inspire the arts, including the craft work of Morris, the interest in the Orient as seen through the paintings of James McNeil Whistler and his architect friend's Colcutt and Beardsley. In Scotland there was a renewed interest in Celtic art and symbolism. Mackintosh designed some very unorthodox furniture in the Art Nouveau style, and his chairs in particular are some of the most unusual to be found of this period. Instead of adopting the naturalistic shape seen in Europe, his chairs are very upright. Some of his chairs are over six feet high with oval insets in pierced patterned squares. They were often painted white and upholstered with linen stencilled with flowers or leaves, or stained and painted black. His chairs have a clarity of line, and fit well into the rather austere

Le Corbusier's luxurious self-adjusting chaise-longue of tubular steel and pony skin, first constructed by Thonet. 1928

"Basculant" chair designed by Le Corbusier. The frame is of chromium plated tubular steel, the back and seat of calf and the strap-like arms of dark hide. 1928

103

Chair that William Morris used as his model.

An unusual nineteenth-century steel stool in the Rococo manner. England. About 1840

interiors that he designed for houses. He is best remembered for designing the Glasgow School of Art.

The Glasgow tea rooms of Miss Cranstone gave Mackintosh an opportunity to engage in complete schemes of interior decoration and furnishing and the designing of some simple chairs to fit in with the general schemes of the Willow Tea Rooms and the Ingram Street Tea Rooms, including a Chinese room and furniture designed to conform with the decoration as a whole. Mackintosh exhibited at the Vienna Secession Exhibition in 1902 and at an exhibition in Turin. His ideas and designs were to have more influence on the Continent than in Britain.

Gleeson White introduced to Europe the Scottish and English styles through *Studio Magazine* in 1897. George Walton, another Scottish designer, had a decoration business in Glasgow designing simple ladder back chairs for the smoking room in one of Miss Cranstone's tea rooms, which could be bought in England and in Europe—and indeed still can.

Charles A. Voysey (1857 to 1941), greatly inspired Art Nouveau artists abroad, designing some very simple chairs in plain oak, the uprights often having, or ending, in small platforms and a heart cut out of the back. He led the movement towards a more rational and stark style for architecture and interiors.

Chapter 7
The Modern Movement

The First World War brought about change in many peoples' lives. On the one hand there was the pre-1914 world which had experienced the war without, it seemed, being aware of any changes, and on the other a new world of young people who hated the thought of another war and who were aware of the great changes caused by it, blaming the last generation. There was, in fact, another industrial revolution happening. On one side the decorative art in the traditional sense was reserved for a limited public, as every piece was hand made, and on the other the industrial art planned by *avant garde* artists and aimed at the largest possible public. By the beginning of the twentieth century new ideas in design were beginning to make themselves felt; styles avoided ornament and relied on simplicity and usefulness, in the adoption of the straight line and use of geometrical forms. In Germany the theories of the architect Muthusius (who maintained that art cannot dissociate itself from the machine) were instrumental in the forming of the Werkbund in 1907 which aimed at the refinement of workmanship and the enhancement of the quality of production, and then after the First War Walter Gropius, a member, formed the Bauhaus in 1919 at Weimar. In America, the architects Frank Lloyd Wright and Louis Sullivan were the first to lay down the principle that form should follow function. These developments helped to bring about the failure of the Art Nouveau movement. When the Art Nouveau style was adopted by industry the result was disastrous and the style was contorted in mass production. The Bauhaus moved to Dessau in Germany in 1925 and was to affect the designs of architecture and furniture all over the

The first chair made of chromium-plated steel tube, designed by Marcel Breuer. Named the *Wassily* after the painter Wassily Kandinsky, it is said to have been inspired by bicycle handlebars.
1925

world—ideas which are still being felt. These ideas on functional design were born at Dessau and when Gropius left Dessau in 1933 with the advent of National Socialism for America, his associates spread all over Europe and particularly America.

Chair design after the First World War was affected in a revolutionary manner and between 1914 and 1939 the whole idea of chair design underwent a great change. Designers abandoned known methods of construction and sought to work with industry and not against it, thus bringing about for the first time good design for the mass public with the aid of the machine and new materials, such as glass, chrome, plywood, plastic and aluminium. It was at the Bauhaus in 1925 that Marcel Breuer, who had been a student at the school, invented the first tubular steel chair known as the *Wassily* chair, after the painter Wassily Kandinsky, who wanted it for his staff house in the new Bauhaus campus. Next, in his *Cantilever* chair he applied architectural form using the "S" shape instead of the usual four legs. Mies Van Der Rohe followed Gropius as the Director of the Bauhaus and is best known for his *Barcelona* Chair, which gained its name from the first annual Exposition held in Barcelona in 1929, where it was displayed at the Barcelona Pavilion. Supporting the sitter's position with cantileverage, it was made of chrome-plated steel bars with leather straps supporting the leather cushions.

The Exhibition in Paris in 1925 gave French designers an opportunity to display new talents and techniques. The history of French Furniture from 1910 to 1930 is the history of French decorative art of the period in all its complexity. Architects had

One of the revolutionary cantilever chairs designed by
Mart Stam in steel tube and leather.
1926

The *MR* chair designed by Mies van der Rohe achieves
its aim in giving comfort without bulkiness. The resilient
frame is of tubular steel and the seat and back are cane.
1926

become interested in furniture designs and were to produce some
interesting examples. The Exposition International des Arts
Decoratifs in Paris in 1925 gave its name to the 1925 style,
or *Art Moderne*; twenty countries exhibited, including America,
Britain and Germany, displaying examples of modern and
industrial art. Art Moderne was not all strictly new, despite
its cubist and geometric shapes and was in fact related to the
past since the designers took classical styles and modernised
them. There were two schools of thought, firstly the traditional-
ists who tried to combine ideas from the past with modern ideas,
and secondly the "moderns" who rejected the past completely
and who were trying to create art of the future. The traditionalist
tried to produce highly refined pieces with specially selected
materials. It is difficult to distinguish typical forms since they
varied according to the character of the designer. Emile Jacque
Rhulman was perhaps one of the most famous and was known
for his luxury furniture often constructed out of rare woods.
His chairs were simple and elegant with spindly legs and often
in the style of the First Empire. Towards the end of his life he
made use of chromed metal. Frances Jourdain was the first
decorator in France to tackle the problem of making the most
of the increasingly restricted space, and he was determined to
produce furniture at a low price for the general public. His
chairs show this in their simplicity as they are completely
undecorated and were constructed on geometrical lines. Robert
Mallet Stevens, foremostly an architect, thought of furniture
in terms of interior volume and introduced metal and painted
chrome-plated tubing. The Swiss-born architect, Charles

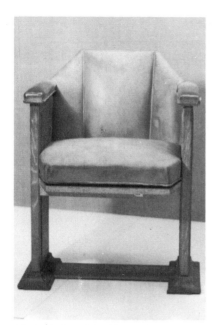

Chair designed by Sir Ambrose Heal
in 1928. Oak, upholstered in
natural hide, made by Heal & Sons
in 1929

The first light standardised wood furniture developed by the Finnish
architect Alvar Aalto for the Paimio Sanatorium.
1930

Edouard Jenneret, called Le Corbusier, and his partners Pierre
Jenneret his cousin and Charlotte Perriand designed objects
for the service of man and not for the decorative arts. In 1927
he designed chairs and tables of various types which were
manufactured by Thonet, in tubing, metal and glass, the most
well known being the reclining chair designed in 1927; this
was a self-adjustable chaise-longue of tubular steel and is perhaps
the most relaxing chair ever designed.

England in the early 1920s lagged behind the rest of Europe
in chair design. Mass-produced reproduction Chippendale,
Jacobean and Queen Anne styles found a place in many homes,
a fashion which was to last for many years, and still does today.
Many pieces were made in completely different scale from their
originals. The age of the "new poor", the "bright young things"
and the "jazz age" are all names given to the 1920s. The young
moderns during this period adopted a nameless style, a fashion
for machine-made "antiques" which had never existed. Interest
was rife in modern painters and the Impressionists and in Matisse
and Picasso and their followers. The Russian Ballet and its
then very modern décor was an obsession with the avant-garde
of the day. But with all these ideas, good furniture design lagged
far behind, except for a few craftsmen among whom Sir
Ambrose Heal and Sir Gordon Russell who were producing
some well-designed chairs in the traditional style. Heal combined
both craftsmanship and quality in his chairs, both machine and
hand made, often of plain stained wood and including lattice
backs. Russell formed a family business in the Cotswolds
where fine quality pieces were produced and still are today.

Brno chair designed by Mies van der Rohe for a private house in Brno, Czechoslovakia, now a children's hospital. Steel bar frame with leather upholstery. 1930

Arm chair designed by Marcel Breuer as part of a suite which won an international competition for aluminium furniture. The slats were intended to carry loose upholstered cushioning. 1933

He followed Ernest Gimson's footsteps designing simple ladder-backed rush-seated chairs. Both Heal and Russell helped to guide Britain into the modern movement of the 1930s. At the end of the 1920s upholstered arm chairs and sofas became squarer and chunkier in shape; arm chairs had wide flat arms on which ash trays, drinks and books could be placed.

Ernest Gimson (1864 to 1920) during the late nineteenth century abandoned a career of architecture to set up a work-shop with Ernest and Sidney Barnsley in Broadway in the Cotswolds, where for a few years they worked together producing simple furniture of their own design. In 1903 a move was made to Sapperton, near Cirencester, to an Elizabethan house called Daneway, where until his death Gimson designed and had made by his craftsmen furniture of an outstanding range and variety. His chair designs were stark and functional using the village craft of making ladder back chairs with rush seats in ash, and designing many strong and graceful variations, which are still made today by Neville Neal at Stockton near Rugby. The emphasis was on the construction of the piece. Gimson influenced many people, including Sir Ambrose Heal and Sir Gordon Russell, and helped to lead to the modern movement in furniture design.

In the early 1930s, the Scandinavian countries brought simplicity to chair design which is still very apparent today. The Finnish architect, Alvar Aalto developed and standardised a form of wood furniture from about 1929 to 1933 for Paimio Sanatorium in Finland, using for the first time wood that was not steamed but bent and pressed into shape by means of a

Cantilever chair designed by Alvar Aalto.
1935

two-piece mould. In 1933 he designed the *Viipuri* chair, wooden and cantilevered, for the Viipuri Library, with mass production in mind. The frame was of laminated birch and the seat and back of plywood.

The twentieth century was one of accelerated change with the result that until recently the inter-war period had been something of a mystery. It was impossible to define the style of the 1920s and 1930s but recent study has revealed a series of complex related styles which over the years between the First World War and 1939 combined to make the international style of today.

Appendix

Acanthus Foliage. Detail of the knee of a cabriole leg.

Cabocmon or "Jewel and Leaf" motif.

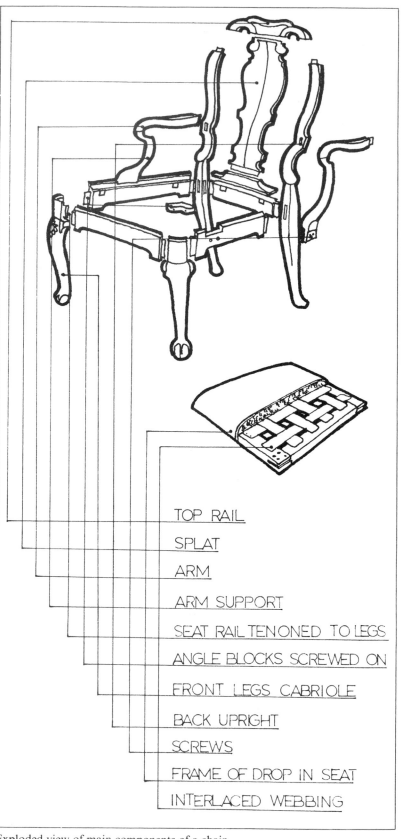

TOP RAIL

SPLAT

ARM

ARM SUPPORT

SEAT RAIL TENONED TO LEGS

ANGLE BLOCKS SCREWED ON

FRONT LEGS CABRIOLE

BACK UPRIGHT

SCREWS

FRAME OF DROP IN SEAT

INTERLACED WEBBING

Exploded view of main components of a chair.

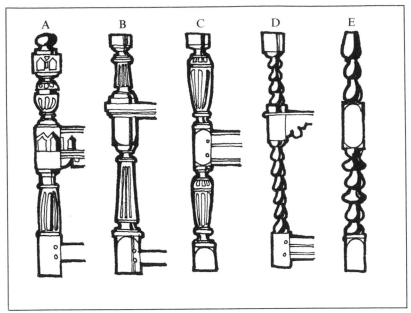

Detail of leg and arm supports of chairs A, B, and C: turned and fluted legs beginning seventeenth century. D and E: ball-turned legs. Middle seventeenth century.

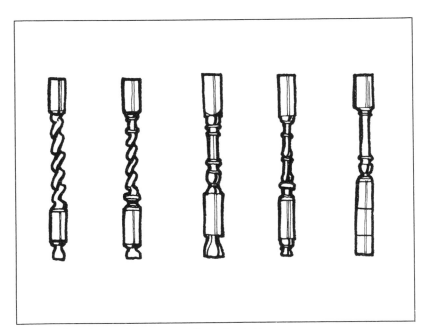

Details of turnings—the supports of gate-leg tables.

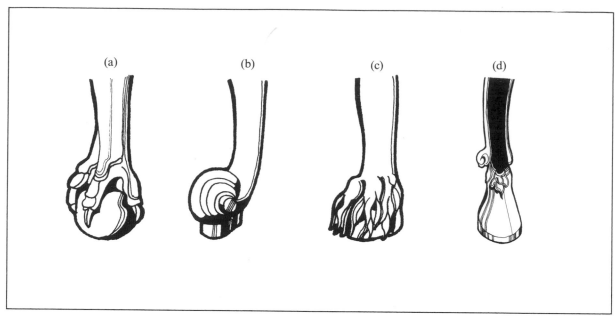

(a) Claw and ball foot. (b) Scroll foot. (c) Paw foot. (d) Hoof foot.

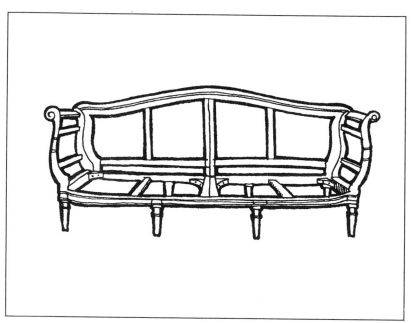

French Royal furniture frame.

French Royal furniture frame.

Bibliography

AUTHOR'S NOTE

Many books on furniture have been published from the seventeenth century onwards. It is not my intention to give a complete reading list here, merely guide lines for further reading. The initials GB and USA indicate whether the book is available in England or America. All the titles listed were in print and available, many in reprinted editions, when this book went to press.

GENERAL

Thomas Chippendale *Gentleman and Cabinet-Maker's Director, GB and USA*
Shirley Spaulding de Voe *Papier Mâché, GB and USA*
H. L. Edlin *What Wood is That? GB and USA*
H. Hayward *World Furniture: A Pictorial History, GB and USA*
G. Grotz *The Furniture Doctor, GB and USA*
George Hepplewhite *Cabinet Maker and Upholsterer's Guide, GB and USA*
Ince and Mayhew *Universal System of Household Furniture, GB and USA*
K. M. McClinton *Antiques in Miniature, GB and USA*
Robert Manwaring *Cabinet and Chair-Maker's Real Friend and Companion, GB and USA*
George Savage *Dictionary of Antiques, GB and USA*
Fakes, Forgeries and Reproductions, GB and USA

ENGLISH FURNITURE

E. Aslin *Nineteenth century English Furniture, GB and USA*
E. Harris *The Furniture of Robert Adam, GB*
P. MacQuoid *History of English Furniture, USA*
C. Musgrave *Regency Furniture, 1800–1830, GB*
R. Symonds *Furniture Making in Seventeenth and Eighteenth Century England, GB*
  Veneered Walnut Furniture, GB and USA

AMERICAN FURNITURE

E. D. and F. Andrews *Shaker Furniture, GB and USA*
Helen Comstock *American Furniture: A Complete Guide to Seventeenth, Eighteenth and early Nineteenth Century Styles, USA*
J. Downs *American Furniture: Queen Anne and Chippendale Periods, GB and USA*
R. H. Kettel *Pine Furniture of early New England, GB and USA*
E. G. Miller *American Antique Furniture, GB and USA*
C. F. Montgomery *American Furniture of the Federal Period, GB and USA*

FRENCH FURNITURE

George Savage *French Decorative Art, GB and USA*
Pierre Verlet *French Royal Furniture, GB and USA*
  French Furniture and Interior Decoration of the Eighteenth Century, GB and USA
F. J. B. Watson *Catalogue of Furniture of the Wallace Collection, GB*
  Louis XVI Furniture, GB

Index

Names of particular styles of chairs are in *italics*